Palgrave Studies in Sub-National Governance

Series Editors
Linze Schaap
Tilburg University
Tilburg, The Netherlands

Jochen Franzke
University of Potsdam
Potsdam, Germany

Hanna Vakkala
Faculty of Social Sciences
University of Lapland
Rovaniemi, Finland

Filipe Teles
University of Aveiro
Aveiro, Portugal

This series explores the formal organisation of sub-national government and democracy on the one hand, and the necessities and practices of regions and cities on the other hand. In monographs, edited volumes and Palgrave Pivots, the series will consider the future of territorial governance and of territory-based democracy; the impact of hybrid forms of territorial government and functional governance on the traditional institutions of government and representative democracy and on public values; what improvements are possible and effective in local and regional democracy; and, what framework conditions can be developed to encourage minority groups to participate in urban decision-making. Books in the series will also examine ways of governance, from 'network governance' to 'triple helix governance', from 'quadruple' governance to the potential of 'multiple helix' governance. The series will also focus on societal issues, for instance global warming and sustainability, energy transition, economic growth, labour market, urban and regional development, immigration and integration, and transport, as well as on adaptation and learning in sub-national government. The series favours comparative studies, and especially volumes that compare international trends, themes, and developments, preferably with an interdisciplinary angle. Country-by-country comparisons may also be included in this series, provided that they contain solid comparative analyses.

Jenny de Fine Licht • David Karlsson
Louise Skoog

Location of Public Services

Legitimacy, Challenges, and Solutions in Sweden

Jenny de Fine Licht 🆔
School of Public Administration
University of Gothenburg
Gothenburg, Sweden

David Karlsson 🆔
School of Public Administration
University of Gothenburg
Gothenburg, Sweden

Louise Skoog 🆔
Political Science
Umeå University
Umeå, Sweden

ISSN 2523-8248　　　　　ISSN 2523-8256　(electronic)
Palgrave Studies in Sub-National Governance
ISBN 978-3-031-64462-7　　ISBN 978-3-031-64463-4　(eBook)
https://doi.org/10.1007/978-3-031-64463-4

© The Editor(s) (if applicable) and The Author(s), under exclusive license to Springer Nature Switzerland AG 2024

This work is subject to copyright. All rights are solely and exclusively licensed by the Publisher, whether the whole or part of the material is concerned, specifically the rights of translation, reprinting, reuse of illustrations, recitation, broadcasting, reproduction on microfilms or in any other physical way, and transmission or information storage and retrieval, electronic adaptation, computer software, or by similar or dissimilar methodology now known or hereafter developed.
The use of general descriptive names, registered names, trademarks, service marks, etc. in this publication does not imply, even in the absence of a specific statement, that such names are exempt from the relevant protective laws and regulations and therefore free for general use.
The publisher, the authors and the editors are safe to assume that the advice and information in this book are believed to be true and accurate at the date of publication. Neither the publisher nor the authors or the editors give a warranty, expressed or implied, with respect to the material contained herein or for any errors or omissions that may have been made. The publisher remains neutral with regard to jurisdictional claims in published maps and institutional affiliations.

This Palgrave Macmillan imprint is published by the registered company Springer Nature Switzerland AG.
The registered company address is: Gewerbestrasse 11, 6330 Cham, Switzerland

If disposing of this product, please recycle the paper.

Preface and Acknowledgement

This book has been written within the project 'The location challenge of public services—equal access to public services and democratic governance in the whole of Sweden', funded by FORMAS, the Swedish Government's research council for sustainable development (2021-02229). It is covered by ethical approval from the Swedish Ethical Review Authority (2022-04557-01).

We declare that we have no known competing financial interests or personal relationships that could have appeared to influence the work reported in this book.

We thank our colleagues at Umeå University and the University of Gothenburg for their constructive comments on the manuscript. Our thanks also go to the reviewers and editors at Palgrave who have made this book possible.

Gothenburg, Sweden	Jenny de Fine Licht
Gothenburg, Sweden	David Karlsson
Umeå, Sweden	Louise Skoog
July 2024	

Terminology: Key Location Concepts

There is some variation in the terminology used in the literature on location of public services. This glossary demonstrates the usage of terms in this book.

Concept	Definition
Public service facility (or unit)	A physical site or building where public services are provided to users (e.g. schools or public indoor swimming pools). More broadly, this encompasses sites where public activities are conducted or public goods are produced, including infrastructure arrangements (e.g. storehouses, bus stops, or energy plants).
Location of public services	The policy area concerned with physical placement of public service facilities.
Location decisions/ decisions on location	The practice of determining the physical placement of public service facilities.
Spatial allocation of public services	The distribution of service facilities over a particular geographical area or polity, determining the general availability of services throughout the entire area. The degree of allocation can be more or less concentrated.
Centralisation/ decentralisation of one or more service facilities	The process of closing service facilities in peripheral places and redirecting users to facilities in more central places, *or* establishing new facilities in peripheral locations where none existed before. (Sometimes referred to as *geographical* centralisation/decentralisation as opposed to centralisation/decentralisation of responsibilities.)
Centralisation/ decentralisation of public service responsibilities (including location decisions)	The relocation of the duty and authority for the provision, funding and location of public services between tiers of government (from lower to higher or vice versa).
LULU	Stands for 'Locally Unwanted Land Use', which in this context refers to a public service facility that is unpopular among local residents. These residents may wish to have it removed if it exists, or prefer to avoid its establishment—at least in their vicinity.
LALU	Stands for 'Locally Attractive Land Use', which in this context is a public service facility desired by the local residents. They would like to retain it if it exists, and if it is absent, they wish for its establishment.

Contents

1 **Introduction** 1
　Location of Wanted and Unwanted Services: The Aim of the Book 2
　What Is the Location Challenge? 4
　A Question of Legitimacy 5
　Why Are Decisions on Location Challenging for Governments? 8
　A Categorisation of Unwanted and Attractive Service Facilities:
　LULUs and LALUs 10
　Location as a Public or Private Concern 13
　A Focus on the Local Political Level 14
　A Decision-Makers' Perspective 15
　The Swedish Case as a Source for Examples 16
　Outline of the Book 17
　References 18

2 **The Centre-Periphery Divide** 21
　What Do We Mean with the Centre-Periphery Divide? 22
　Centralisation and Decentralisation of Public Service Facilities 25
　The Interests of Service Users and Citizens 26
　Public Opinion on Location Issues 32
　To Eat One's Cake and Have It Too 38
　Summary 40
　References 41

3 The Quest for Legitimacy — 45
What Is Legitimacy? — 45
Normative and Empirical Legitimacy — 47
What Drives Legitimacy? A Question of Substance and Process — 49
Evaluating Legitimacy — 54
Summary — 58
References — 58

4 Location in a Multilevel Setting — 61
Local Self-governance Versus National Equity — 62
Multilevel Governance — 65
Public, Private, or Civil Sector Responsibility for Service Provision — 67
The Size of a Polity — 72
Structural Reforms, Amalgamations, and Tensions Within Municipalities — 74
Summary — 76
References — 77

5 Party Conflicts and Political Representation — 81
Party Conflicts Over Public Service Provision and Facility Location — 82
Political Parties and Location Issues — 85
How Do Parties Represent the Opinions of Citizens in Location Issues? — 88
Summary — 93
References — 94

6 Making Decisions on Location — 97
Avoiding Painful Decisions — 98
Conflict or Compromise: Two Models of Democracy — 99
Open or Closed Decision-Making — 101
Public Involvement in Decision-Making — 103
Why Public Participation Is Not Necessarily the Solution — 106
Summary — 109
References — 110

7 **Solutions**	115
Embrace the Location Challenge as a Political Issue	116
Induce Realistic Expectations	118
Secure Knowledge-Based Institutions and Due Administrative Processes	120
Think Creatively Yet Critically About Technical Innovations	121
Extend the Process Beyond the Actual Decision	123
Compensate the Affected	124
Proceed with Caution in Collaborative Arrangements	125
Design Multilevel Systems That Support, Not Undermine, Local Democracy	127
Key Areas for Future Research on the Location Challenge	129
The Decision-Making Perspective	129
Public Opinion Studies	129
Comparisons	130
Location Problems in a Time-Perspective	131
Conceptual and Theoretical Development	132
References	133
Index	137

LIST OF FIGURES

Fig. 1.1	Distance to maternity wards. (*Note:* Pictures produced by and reproduced with permission from *@Inlandsaktivisterna*)	7
Fig. 1.2	Dimensions of location decisions	12
Fig. 2.1	Local citizen interest in relation location of public services	28
Fig. 2.2	Public opinion in Sweden 2022 on the ideological trade-off between centralisation and decentralisation of public services (the c/d-scale), per cent. (Source: The National SOM Survey 2022, $N = 1674$. *Note:* The figure illustrates the distribution of opinions among Swedish individuals regarding the survey question referenced in the figure)	33
Fig. 2.3	Support for political proposals regarding location issues (per cent). (Source: The national SOM survey 2022, $N = 1707–1738$. *Note:* The question was, 'What is your opinion on the following proposals?', and the responses were given on a five-graded scale from very good to very bad proposal. The figure illustrates the percentage who responded very good or rather good proposal. The proposals are sorted according to popularity, with the least popular proposals first)	35
Fig. 2.4	Those who choose to live in rural areas/smaller localities must be prepared for poorer access to services (per cent). (Source: The National SOM Survey 2022. *Note:* The question reads: 'To what extent do you agree that those who choose to live in rural areas/smaller localities must be prepared for poorer access to services?' and responses are indicated on a scale from 1 'Do not agree at all' to 7 'Fully agree'. $N = 1734$)	39

Fig. 4.1 Changes in Swedish politicians' views on self-governance and equality 2008–2019 (balance: positive-negative). (Sources: For national politicians: RDU 2010, 2014, 2019 (see Karlsson, 2018; Öhberg et al., 2022); for local and regional politicians: KOLFU 2008, 2012, 2017 (see Gilljam et al., 2010; Karlsson & Gilljam, 2014; Karlsson, 2017). Adapted from Karlsson (2022a). *Note*: The figure presents a balance measure, specifically the proportion of politicians who believe the cited proposals are very bad or fairly bad subtracted from the proportion who consider it fairly good or very good)   64

Fig. 4.2 Swedish public opinion on wind power issues. (*Note*: Results from the National SOM survey 2022 (Axelsson et al., 2023). In the Swedish Context, 'the state' refers to the government and authorities at the national level)   72

Fig. 5.1 Distribution of responses to questions on spatial allocation of services (the c/d-scale) and support for preserving schools in small villages and rural areas among citizens and politicians at national, regional, and local levels (percentage). (Sources: National politicians: the RDU survey 2014 $N = 265$ (Karlsson & Lindstrand, 2018); regional politicians ($N = 1074$) and local politicians ($N = 7444$) from the KOLFU survey 2017 (Karlsson, 2017); citizens ($N = 1674$) from The National SOM survey 2022 (de Fine Licht et al., 2023). *Note*: The figure illustrates the distribution of responses for two survey questions. The first question related to the c/d-scale was: 'Regarding the location of services, there is sometimes talk of a political dimension between: Those who want centralised public services (for the sake of efficiency and quality), and those who want decentralised public services (to promote equitable access to services everywhere). Where would you personally place yourself on a centralisation-decentralisation scale?' The responses were given on a 0–10 scale from definitely for centralisation to definitely for decentralisation. The second question was presented as a proposal 'Preserve schools in rural/less populated areas' and the responses were given on a scale from 1 'very bad' to 5 'very good' proposal)   90

Fig. 5.2 Policy congruence between citizens and politicians by party affiliation regarding spatial allocation of services (the c/d-scale) and support for preserving schools in small villages and rural areas (mean values). (*Note*: For the formulation of survey questions and sources for the three surveys, refer to the note on Fig. 5.1. In this figure, responses are represented as mean values on the c/d scale (0 representing definitely for centralisation, 10 representing definitely for decentralisation) and the question regarding preserving schools (1 being a very bad proposal, 5 being a very good proposal), with a grey vertical line indicating the neutral position on each scale. Values are categorised according to party affiliation for the eight national parties (*L* Liberals, *M* Moderates [conservative], *KD* Christian Democrats, *SD* Sweden Democrats [nationalists], *MP* Greens, *V* Left Party [socialists], *S* Social Democrats, *C* Centre Party [agrarians])) 91

Fig. 6.1 A snow dump. (*Note:* This is one of four snow dumps in Umeå, a mid-sized city in the north of Sweden. Photo by Louise Skoog) 106

LIST OF TABLES

Table 2.1	Correlation between pinions on different service location proposals (Pearson's *r*)	36
Table 4.1	Distribution of responsibilities in three public service sectors between tiers of government in Sweden	67

CHAPTER 1

Introduction

'The maternity Ward in Lycksele is closed—Heavily pregnant Emma is forced to drive 300 kilometres.' So reads the headline in 2023 of a leading newspaper in Sweden, *Dagens Nyheter* (Kejerhag, 2023), signalling seriousness and justified concern. Emma, who lives on a farm in the inner parts of northern Sweden, is nine months pregnant. She estimates that if everything goes well, it will take her four hours to drive to Umeå, where the nearest maternity ward is placed. 'It feels really scary,' she tells the journalist, in a reportage illustrated by pictures of beautiful but heavily snow-covered landscapes.

The background is that the maternity ward in Lycksele, an inland town in northern Sweden with about 12,000 inhabitants, closed in January 2023 for an indefinite period due to difficulties in recruiting qualified staff. In effect, pregnant women in the inner areas of Sweden must travel to the coastal cities of Umeå or Skellefteå to give birth.

People living in the inner parts of the region are upset and channel their discontent in different ways. One example of a particularly active platform is the Instagram account '@Inlandsaktivisterna' (The Inland Activists). Most of their work is focused on spreading a positive image of life in the sparsely populated areas, such as posting photos of ski slopes, swimming in lakes, fishing, barbecue evenings, and the tranquillity of nature. They reject the sometimes-gloomy picture of rural areas as boring and sad,

© The Author(s), under exclusive license to Springer Nature Switzerland AG 2024
J. de Fine Licht et al., *Location of Public Services*, Palgrave Studies in Sub-National Governance,
https://doi.org/10.1007/978-3-031-64463-4_1

arguing that they have chosen to live in the remote areas of inland Sweden because of its beauty and potential for a high-quality life. However, the main problem in their eyes is that community service gradually has disappeared. They are critical of how authorities in the Region of Västerbotten (the county) provide services to the inland parts of the region in general and of the maternity ward in Lycksele in particular. According to them, the region has not done enough to resolve the situation: 'We are also paying taxes, but often feel unfairly treated. The urban norm prevails,' an activist argues (Österlind, 2023).

The Region of Västerbotten, which is the governing body responsible for healthcare services in the area, asserts that it has tried its best to find a solution. The ambition has been to open the maternity ward in Lycksele again as soon as a sufficient number of personnel have been recruited, but it has proven difficult to convince midwives and doctors to take on positions in the small and remotely situated towns and villages. Patients who have to travel long distances will be compensated for the expenses and they may receive free hotel accommodation.

But hotel is not an option for Emma and her family, she claims. 'We have seven hens, a rooster, three dogs, and a cat. Who will take care of them and for how long? We can't just leave everything' (Kejerhag, 2023). At the same time, there is no quick solution on the table. 'There is no possibility of opening before we have found [enough] staff,' says head of the regional hospital department (Eriksson, 2023).

Location of Wanted and Unwanted Services: The Aim of the Book

The case of the maternity ward in Lycksele serves as an example of the complex challenge in determining physical location for public services. Such decisions can give rise to conflicts between deeply held personal and institutional values and interests, where political, economic, practical, and health-related considerations all come into play.

Some manifestations of government presence are generally viewed positively by local communities. Physical establishment of services such as schools, bus stops, elder care facilities, clinics, public libraries, and, as in the case above, maternity wards represent the official societal framework and welfare ambitions, and citizens often welcome the placement of these in their area, and they cherish and defend existing services against any threat of removal (e.g. Pierson, 1996; Starke, 2006). Debates regarding reduced local availability of these services tend to evoke strong reactions from citizens, expressing both practical and emotional concerns about being 'left behind' by public authorities, often leading to heated protests.

Other signs of government presence in an area are typically seen as negative to the community, at least in people's immediate neighbourhood. This category may include homes for juvenile delinquents, waste and recycling stations, airports, wind farms, prisons, or temporary housing for refugees. In contrast to the previously mentioned cases, these services and public facilities tend to activate feelings of fear, disgust, or frustration rather than of community belonging, and to generate citizen protests when they are planned and placed at a particular location (e.g. Hunold & Young, 1998; Aldrich, 2016). A wind farm, for example, is often valued in general terms for its potential to produce clean and renewable energy, but people also tend to regard them as disturbing when in their own sight. Even if not providing services in a traditional way—a prisoner, for example, would probably not feel comfortable with that description—we will refer also to facilities that provide goods and perform tasks for the general public well-being as services.

The location of both wanted and unwanted services poses dilemmas to those ultimately responsible for making the decisions. At the same time, decisions on location are unavoidable. As Christopher Pollitt (2012) has put it, 'government has a face and a place': it needs to be visibly and physically present at different locations in its territory. Services must be provided, and goods need to be generated, but finances as well as laws and quality demands place boundaries on how close to each citizen these facilities can be placed. Similarly, unwanted facilities that are beneficial for the greater good of the community or even country need a physical placement, and geography and regulations places boundaries on possible options. Technical innovation, digitalisation, and creative collaborations can be parts of solutions in some cases but will not make the problem away completely. Addressing these decisions is a complex task for public representatives, involving considerations of accessibility, equality, efficiency, and fairness. How these challenges are navigated speaks volumes about the state of our democracy.

This book aims to offer a comprehensive introduction to the challenges associated with decisions on location of public services, with a specific focus on how such complex and at times painful decisions can gain public acceptance. We will not present definitive solutions to the problems.

Rather, by presenting an overview of perspectives and considerations involved in location decisions, our goal is to establish a framework for analysing the decision-making processes related to the placement or removal of governmental services and their facilities within a democratic context. This means that we will formulate questions as well as potential solutions and add complexity as well as provide orientation. Our hope is that the framework will speak to both emerging researchers in the field and to practitioners working with issues relating to location of services, who are searching for conceptual tools and perspectives to guide their work. Throughout the book we will primarily use illustrative examples and vignettes from the perspective of Swedish local government, but the challenges of location politics are universal, and the available toolbox is similar in many contexts and tiers of government, at least in liberal democracies.

The remainder of this introductory chapter will provide a basis for the forthcoming discussions. We will explain what we mean by a location problem and why such problems are particularly difficult to manage in a democratic context. We will also provide an initial classification of governmental facilities, taking their relative attractiveness to the local community as a point of departure. Furthermore, we will, in this chapter, elaborate on our choice to focus on the local level of government and introduce the case of Sweden, which provides most of our illustrative examples. We will conclude by providing an overview of the remaining chapters in the book.

What Is the Location Challenge?

Throughout this book, we will focus on decisions and situations when public authorities—political leaders and/or other public officials—determine *where* public services will be available and public goods will be generated, and accordingly, *where* facilities and institutions providing services and goods will be physically present. To decide on location of public services is often synonymous with 'placing' and 'siting' of public facilities—both terms are commonly used in the literature. However, we will primarily use the term 'location' to signal the inherent political nature of the activity. The focus on 'where' in this context also means, for example, that a decision to provide library service online, or by an itinerant bus, may constitute a location decision as it implicitly rule out the use of a physical library branch in a local community (Kantur, 2024). Further, the focus on both public services and public goods means that decisions on the location of public services may include both facilities that the citizens can visit to receive a benefit or burden (such as a school or a prison) and those that produce goods for the society (such as a wind farm or nuclear plant).

Location decisions are, of course, not a new phenomenon. Even in historically ancient times, the powers that be needed to decide where to place public buildings and activities, taking into consideration the distance people would have to travel to visit the market, seek justice in court, pay their taxes, or visit their place of worship. Moreover, most location decisions are unavoidable, even though some political actors certainly try to avoid or at least delay unpopular decisions. For example, the closure of facilities in poor and shrinking rural areas can be countered by ambitious strategies aimed at promoting tourism or attracting companies with substantial economic resources, thereby altering the demographic trajectory and/or increasing incomes (e.g. Syssner, 2020). Similarly, many try to avoid conflicts over unwanted facilities by placing them out of sight for as many people as possible. Nevertheless, even within an unrealistically generous budget, aspects such as legal restrictions, quality demands, and availability of skilled personnel will place boundaries on the potential density of services, as well as on their possible siting.

Location decisions take place at all tiers of government: local, regional, national, and to some extent even supra-national (such as the EU level). Further, they often concern and activate tensions between the central administration of a country and its rural areas, but also between urban and rural areas within the same region or municipality, and even between areas of the same city. Political decision-making on location of public services is influenced by centre-periphery dynamics, where the places and people at the centre tend to have much more access to service than those in the periphery. This dynamic is often most visible and discussed in issues where the interests and values of urban and rural populations clash. However, the centre-periphery divide transcends a simplified urban-rural dichotomy and can also be found, for example, between more and less resourceful parts of the same city.

A Question of Legitimacy

A central argument of this book is that decisions on where and how to locate public services are at the heart of what politics actually means. Who gets what, when and how, is a classic definition of 'politics' by Lasswell (1936), which is exactly what decisions on the distribution of valued and less valued services are about.

That decisions on location are political does not mean that all instances of the decision-making process are handled by politicians. Depending on context, public administrators are, for example, often the ones compiling facts from experts, investigating different alternatives, communicating with organised interests and the public, and suggesting solutions. In many cases, especially in smaller municipalities where a few individuals are involved in many different tasks and issues, administrators are also the ones identifying a problem and drawing the politicians' attention to it (Erlingsson et al., 2022; Skoog & Svensson, 2023). Moreover, which decisions that are even possible to make are highly dependent on external factors such as presence and directions of local industries. That location decisions are political does, however, mean that even though these decisions can be delegated to administrators or outsourced to external actors, politicians are normally held accountable for the outcomes. If the access to service facilities is perceived as inadequate or the proximity of unwanted facilities is considered too close, politicians may face criticism and blame from the public.

Moreover, we argue that decisions on locations are fundamental to *democratic legitimacy*. To be successful over time, authorities need to ensure that their decisions and policies are accepted or at least tolerated by the citizens (e.g. Tyler, 2006). As public services are the primary interface between citizens and government, public facilities for service constitute a prime site at which attitudes and opinions concerning government are formed (Pollitt, 2012, p. 11). Giving all citizens what they demand in terms of service accessibility while always avoiding placing unwanted facilities near those who object is, however, not an option. Governments, and in particular municipalities that operate in close proximity to citizens, need to find policies and processes that can be perceived as legitimate by at least a majority of the population.

In a democracy, we also tend to prefer that citizens accept decisions *for the right reasons.* In a system where the people are supposed to govern themselves, we do not want people to have blind faith in authorities or uncritically accept everything that is decided (e.g. Norris, 2022). Rather, a healthy critical citizenry is an asset for governments, as it can bring different perspectives to the table, generate creative solutions to problems, force decision-makers to gather critical information and sharpen their arguments, and, ultimately, demand accountability if outcomes are insufficient. Therefore, finding ways to channel the dedication of citizens that is attached to manifestations of government presence in the local community into political problem-solving is vital for the future of democracy.

> **A Case of Place-Based Activism**
> These maps are examples of how The Inland Activists (@inlandsaktivisterna) strive to spread their messages on social media. The first map illustrates the distance to the nearest maternity ward that women in some parts of northern Sweden must travel. The second map demonstrates the travelling distance that women in the capital area of Stockholm would face if they had the same distance to a maternity ward as women in inland northern Sweden. The purpose of these maps is to evoke a sense of absurdity among people living in urban areas by showing them the equivalent distances in Southern Sweden (Fig. 1.1).
>
>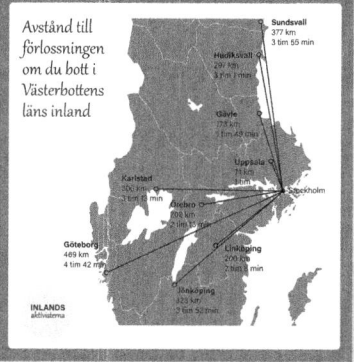
>
> **Fig. 1.1** Distance to maternity wards. (*Note:* Pictures produced by and reproduced with permission from *@Inlandsaktivisterna*)

Why Are Decisions on Location Challenging for Governments?

At a glance, location decisions might look fairly straightforward. If you, for example, have a certain number of citizens who need a specific type of service within a reasonable distance, you can calculate the rational amount of facilities needed as well as their spatial allocation (e.g. Hodgart, 1978), and adjust according to present resource constraints. If the size of the population decreases in a rural area, the strictly rational decision might be to relocate services accordingly by, for example, centralising operations from a shrinking village to a larger town or city. Similarly, if you need to locate a hazardous facility, you pick the site where it will serve its purpose while disturbing as few inhabitants as possible.

However, location issues are rarely so simple and rational. Distance to service is, for example, not merely an objective question of kilometres (Hawthorne & Kwan, 2012; de Fine Licht et al., 2023). The importance of distance is highly dependent on, for instance, whether people have access to a car or public transport. How people perceive the distance may also be dependent on how they perceive the quality of the service in an area or the safety of the nearest route to a facility.

Moreover, it is important to consider that people form strong emotional connections to places (Agnew, 1987). The prosperity and future of the places where people live and where social relations and interactions happen means a lot to them. Facilities and institutions in their home area gain symbolic meaning (Christiaanse & Haartsen, 2017). Further, the history of a place matters: if you lose something that has been there for some time, like a local school or an undisturbed horizon of a beautiful landscape, the loss is often far more painful than the experience if the facility was never there in the first place.

As we will show throughout the book, public decision-makers—political leaders supported by public officials—need to navigate a highly complex landscape involving ideological, practical, as well as emotional considerations, in order to arrive at a decision on where to locate a public service. Since location decisions are political, they naturally evoke political conflicts. Political representatives, who may themselves be highly emotionally involved in the local community, must handle tensions within their own political party as well as between parties and coalition partners.

Political parties are in themselves guided by ideology but also by electoral and relational concerns. Moreover, they often have to process complicated and perhaps contradictory advice from public officials or experts on technical solutions, predictions of future population development, and risks of negative side effects. Decisions regarding the location of a certain type of service can easily, and sometimes unintentionally, affect the availability of services in several other areas. Will the closing of a local school, for example, cause families with children to move away from the village, thereby reducing the customer base for the local grocery store, the voluntary workforce needed to sustain the local sports club, the number of visitors required to motivate the library branch, or the number of passengers to justify a detour for the bus running between the larger cities in the area?

Further, even if the political parties manage to arrive at a decision—whether majoritarian or consensual—they still must navigate their relation to the public. Formally, the legitimacy of policy decisions in representative democracy is based on citizens' opportunity to choose their decision-makers in recurrent elections. Between elections, political representatives have the right—and responsibility—to make decisions on the issues that arise on the agenda, for instance on the location of services. Formal power is, however, not everything. This is particularly evident in many situations of location decisions, where members of the public often do not settle with the argument that they had their chance to influence a couple of years ago, especially not after an election campaign that likely revolved around other issues than, for instance, the potential closure of a cherished library branch.

As location decisions tend to evoke strong emotions, there is a great risk of heated conflicts and delayed processes whenever the topic is on the table (e.g. Fredriksson & Moberg, 2018; Larsson Taghizadeh, 2016; Wolf & Van Dooren, 2018; Proctor & Simmons, 2000; Pepermans & Loots, 2013). While considerable hope has been placed in finding procedures for public participation and influence as a means to overcome disputes, experiences show that it is not always easy to make people discuss and consider options that they believe are not to their advantage, especially if they perceive their community's future to be at risk. All in all, making legitimate decisions on the location of public services is among the most challenging issues that governments deal with.

A Categorisation of Unwanted and Attractive Service Facilities: LULUs and LALUs

While services can take place in many forms, including digital solutions and technical innovations, the controversies regarding location of services often imply that physical service facilities are, in one way or another, involved. The broad literature on planning and land use identifies some facilities as 'Locally Unwanted Land Use' (LULU) (e.g. Been, 1992; Grimes & Esaiasson, 2014). This refers facilities that people prefer to have at a distance from where they live, such as waste management services or prisons. LULUs are at times hazardous, like industrial garbage facilities, but are sometimes 'just' unpleasant, for example because they reduce the beauty of a place. In either case, decisions on where to locate LULUs tend to generate tension and political conflicts. The reactions that these facilities tend to evoke have been termed the NIMBY, that is the Not-In-My-Backyard-syndrome, referring to 'the protectionist attitudes of and oppositional tactics adopted by community groups facing an unwelcome development in their neighborhood' (Dear, 1992, p. 288). The concepts of LULU and NIMBY are related, but where 'NIMBY' emphasises the personal opposition of individuals or groups to a specific location decision in their local area, 'LULU' in this context represents more generally the types of services that are typically unwanted, regardless of where they may be located. We prefer the use of LULU as the more general term in this book, even in cases where both NIMBY and LULU might be applicable.

Citizen protests against LULUs are often understandable and a sign that people care about their community, but these conflicts can grow too extreme and generate a society so ridden with conflict that communities are divided and political stability is threatened. A particular worry has been that LULUs will be deliberately located in areas that are already suffering from political, economic, and social inequities since wealthier neighbourhoods are more successful in mobilising against unwanted facilities (e.g. Greenberg, 1993). Another concern is that protesters will move beyond the regular democratic mechanisms for influence and engage in violent actions or threats against public figures.

In absence of an established term for the opposite of LULUs, that is cases of *wanted* service facilities, we will, in this book, introduce the concept of LALU ('Locally-Attractive-Land-Use'). This is a term we will use for services that generally are regarded as positive assets for a community, like schools or libraries. In contrast to the LULU cases above—where the initial location of a service tends to generate conflict—LALUs often become contentious when facing threats of closure, removal, or downsizing. The reactions that LALUs under threat generate have sometimes been termed NOOMBYism (Not-Out-Of-My-Backyard) (Stewart & Aitken, 2015), but this somewhat convoluted term does not seem to be frequently used.

The nature of LALUs and LULUs should be considered on a scale rather than as a dichotomy. Some public services are more attractive—or unattractive—than others. And what is attractive is not only a matter of individual taste but also of the contextual history of a place. A prison, for example, is often regarded as a LULU, but for an isolated municipality with shrinking population, the potential establishment of a prison within its territory can imply job opportunities that outweigh the fact that the service itself may be perceived as uncomfortable (Pettersson, 2023). Similarly, while the location of wind turbines is a heatedly debated issue in Sweden (and many other countries), public opinion in neighbouring Denmark is much more positive, even among those who reside fairly close to the turbines. Suggested reasons are that Danes have had a longer time to get used to the turbines, but also that Denmark has succeeded in establishing a much more positive narrative surrounding wind power (Törnwall, 2023).

Alongside the distinctions between LALUs and LULUs, there are also services that are *more* or *less necessary* for a locality to function and for its residents to live there. A school may, for example, be a LALU of high importance for a community—providing both education, job opportunities, and acting as community hubs (Cedering & Wihlborg, 2020). Conversely, a public indoor swimming pool (PISP) may indeed be highly attractive and provide a service that, while beneficial and popular among the community, is arguably less necessary for the everyday lives of citizens as a school. In the Swedish case, several municipalities lack public indoor swimming pools, but all of them are required by law to provide schools. Similarly, a waste disposal facility may be a LULU that people do not want to be near their own home, but it may still be regarded as necessary for a community to thrive. In contrast, public opinion regarding the necessity of some services, for example a particular type of power plant, may be more of a political preference. For some, a specific form of power plant, such as a nuclear facility or a wind turbine, might be deemed unnecessary regardless of its location, as there are other, more acceptable options for energy production.

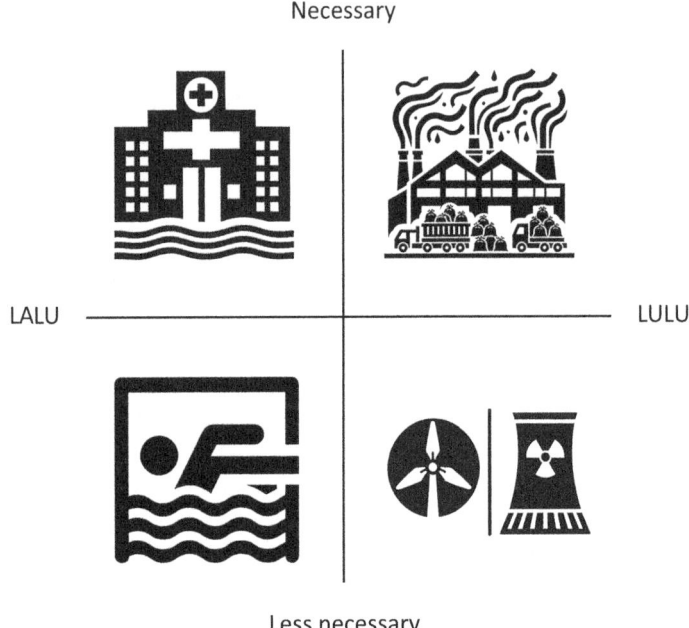

Fig. 1.2 Dimensions of location decisions

By contrasting the LALU-LULU dimension with a necessary-unnecessary dimension of public service facilities, we can create a model that presents a schematic representation of location problems. This model can help us analysing the relative 'hotness' of different location issues (see Fig. 1.2).

Generally speaking, we would expect decisions on location of services, infrastructure, and facilities to be most controversial in the top left corner of this model, when LALUs perceived as necessary are threatened, and in the low right corner, when a LULU that the public view as less necessary is proposed. This default assumption should, however, be treated with caution. There are certainly cases where a LALU that to an outsider could be seen as unnecessary generates strong community responses in a context where it has gained historic and symbolic dignity. Similarly, a LULU deemed necessary by objective measures can also provoke intense opposition when combined with a strong NIMBY logic: 'yes, we as a society need it, but not where I can see or smell it.' This situation is particularly likely if a service or facility can be perceived as unsafe or toxic.

Location as a Public or Private Concern

Another complicating factor whether discussing LALUs or LULUs is that services may be perceived as a *public* concern and responsibility to a greater or lesser extent. Which types of services that are public, and which are private, is not just something that varies legally between countries, but also has to do with political ideology and public opinion. In some cases, government is formally responsible for a particular service. In Sweden, as in many other countries, this is the case with primary and secondary education. Although there are also privately owned schools in Sweden, these are funded by taxpayers' money, regulated by national laws, and subjected to oversight from public authorities—meaning that schools are never entirely a private matter. In total, about one in six Swedish pupils attends a private primary school, and one in three attends a private secondary school. However, regardless of presence of private schools, local governments are still responsible for providing education to all children, irrespectively of where in the municipality they live. Although the existence of privately owned schools complicates the situation, the formal municipal responsibility for schools (both municipal and private) makes questions of accountability, blame, and credit comparatively straightforward. However, as we will see later on, a multilevel system of government involving both national and local participation can introduce a fair amount of confusion.

In other cases, public actors have the role as both providers, and enablers and facilitators. This can, for example, be the case with energy production. In the Swedish case, approximately half of the energy production is attributed to public facilities, with municipalities owning 13 per cent. While some municipalities are involved in setting up new wind turbines and solar power parks, the majority of these new energy ventures rely on private providers. In those cases, the role of local authorities is primarily to grant land use permissions to energy companies. Their direct influence over these operations is thereby limited; they cannot mandate where private companies should build but can use their veto to halt planned constructions, leading to a more uncertain decision-making environment.

Finally, in some cases of service production, public actors are not formally responsible at all but are still, willingly or unwillingly, involved. In Sweden, the establishment and running of grocery stores is, for example, a matter for the private market. There are no legal possibilities for public actors to sell groceries. At the same time, Sweden is a country with vast areas of sparsely populated countryside. Local grocery stores are—along with other private market suppliers like petrol stations—essential for rural living conditions (Strandh, 2023). With increased urbanisation, more and more local providers of key services are finding it hard to continue their business in certain regions, resulting in so-called resource deserts in rural areas (Carson et al., 2022). When voters witness service providers increasingly abandoning their region, many will not see it as an isolated event but indicative of a broader societal decline. As a result, voters often direct their blame towards public and political actors, criticising them for the neglect of rural areas. The core issue for politicians, both local and national, is that despite lacking formal authority to operate businesses like grocery stores, they face voter condemnation for their closures and the perceived decline of rural life. This criticism can, of course, become a significant concern for politicians who depend on voter support. This makes location decisions even more complex. The well-being and sustainability of a place are potentially much larger questions than the isolated decision on the location of a particular facility, and the tools at hand are not always sufficient.

A Focus on the Local Political Level

In this book, our main focus is on location decisions made at local political level, as well as on aspects of location that depend on the relationship between national and local tiers of government.

There are several reasons for this local emphasis. Primarily, all location decisions are inherently local, irrespective of the tier of government responsible for the public service in question. All service facilities are placed in a locality, and the presence or absence of these facilities affects the people who live there. At national level, decisions typically concern general values and directions, and prioritisations between large groups of citizens, including determining the boundaries of the welfare state and moral issues of freedom and rights. Such scope may allow more room for grand ideas but can also enable politicians to distance themselves—both physically and emotionally—from those immediately affected by their decisions. At local level, the focus of our study, policy issues tend to be both more immediate and comprehensible to individuals than policy decisions at the national level (e.g. Nabatchi & Amsler, 2014). Rather than targeting fairly anonymous groups of citizens, location decisions at this level pertain to organising of the actual local community and managing the effects on the individuals who live in it.

Moreover, local politicians often reside in the locality affected by their decisions. This means that local politicians are personally subjected to both the outcomes of their own decisions and to the reactions from potentially resentful or even hostile citizens to a larger extent. In addition, citizens are likely to feel that decisions are important to them and might find it comparatively easy to locate and confront a responsible local politician. Taken together, we can expect that local politicians are likely to have a more personal relationship with both the location and the citizens, which probably influences their perceptions of what constitutes a difficult decision.

However, even though our primary focus in this book is on the local political level, we must acknowledge the influence of national priorities that set the framework within which local governments operate. The interplay of centralisation and decentralisation between levels of society, coupled with demands for equitable services, significantly shapes local policy. Moreover, in a contemporary welfare state, local politics are a vital component of the national welfare system. This interconnection implies that the implementation of local services is reflective of the broader functioning of the welfare model in a more general sense. Additionally, the placement of services run by national authorities such as prisons (LULU) or train stations (LALU) inevitably occurs within the confines of municipal boundaries, eliciting local political responses from citizens. For most people, the multilevel system's formal distribution of responsibility is not their primary frame of reference; rather, they perceive it as the 'state' making decisions that directly impact them.

A Decision-Makers' Perspective

While focusing on location of public services at local level, we adopt a primarily top-down approach—from the perspective of decision-makers—to examine the location challenge of public services. This means that although there exists an important body of literature problematising location issues from the perspective of citizen mobilisation, grassroots protests, and social movements, we address this issue from a system-level perspective. This place particular emphasises on public authorities—political representatives and public officials—and their considerations and strategies. However, it is crucial to note that this does not in any way diminish the importance of the citizen perspective. As will become clear, the unique situations, needs, perceptions, experiences, and communication methods of the public play a pivotal role in explaining why location problems pose particular challenges for (local) governments and why the handling of these decisions is crucial for the legitimacy of the democratic system.

We also adopt the representative model of liberal democracy as a given starting point. This form of democracy, as prescribed by the constitutions of most Western countries including Sweden, sets the formal framework for the decision-making processes we examine. In doing so, we consider certain aspects of a political system as inherent, both in terms of norms and empirical observations. These include the expectation of regular free and fair elections, freedom of speech, and a functioning rule of law. We also assume a certain level of public responsibility for welfare services. Within the representative model, there exists considerable room for variation. For instance, the extent of public influence between elections ranges from practically non-existent to nearly all-encompassing but formal. Likewise, questions about a (local) government's responsibilities and the extent to which these can be delegated to civil society and private entrepreneurs are highly influenced by cultural and political factors. We will not, however, delve into discussions about radically different models of democracy, such as direct democracy.

The Swedish Case as a Source for Examples

The challenges in location of public services are both timeless and universal. The issue arises in governments at all tiers of government and in all countries. However, this book will focus on the Swedish case, primarily utilising Swedish local government data and examples for illustrating the problems discussed.

Sweden is often described as a Social democratic welfare regime with historically high ambitions on geographically based equality when it comes to public service, captured in the slogan 'let the whole country thrive', used by political parties from left to right. At the same, Sweden is area-wise a large country with significant contrasts between growing urban areas and shrinking rural ones (Syssner, 2020). Although politically, there is no strong urban-rural polarisation (Erlingsson et al., 2021; Karlsson & Skoog, 2023), as we will explore in this book, people living in the countryside tend to have less faith in the functioning of the political institutions.

The local government systems of the Nordic countries—including Sweden—deviate in several significant respects from the typical characteristics of multilevel systems in other parts of the world (Sellers et al., 2020; Lidström, 2015). Compared to other countries, Swedish local governments have an extensive local autonomy (Ladner et al., 2016) and major political responsibilities for welfare services—for everything from education, elder care infrastructure, to leisure activities—and they also set their own tax rate (Sellers et al., 2020; Montin, 2015). This also means that how these tasks are managed varies across Swedish municipalities. And although all municipalities are subject to the same legislation and have the same responsibilities, they are not equally equipped in terms of capacity, to carry out the tasks assigned to them by central level. The challenges that municipalities face can also vary widely: some are small and shrinking, while others are large and growing rapidly. This not only creates different problems to address but also different opportunities to resolve them.

The geographical size of Swedish municipalities varies significantly. From Kiruna (Sweden's largest municipality by geographical measures) that covers 20,553 square kilometres—making it larger than four EU member states: Slovenia, Malta, Cyprus, and Luxembourg—to Sundbyberg (Sweden's smallest municipality area wise) that only covers 9 square kilometres. Rural municipalities that have large geographical areas, especially those with a low and/or decreasing population, face significant challenges in upholding functional services and viable communication between different parts of their municipality. This is evident, for example, in home care services, schools, social care, and snow removal. Both geographical area and population size thus have significant implications for municipal operations.

The fact that Swedish municipalities possess very strong autonomy, a significant responsibility for producing welfare services, and a political system wherein political parties play a predominant role in governance within a system based on parliamentary principles (Montin, 2015; Gilljam & Karlsson, 2015; Skoog, 2019), means that the political dynamics within Swedish local governments in many ways mirror those of much larger polities at regional or even national levels in other countries. Additionally, Sweden faces multiple geographic and demographic challenges that underscore the significance of location politics.

In sum, these characteristics make Sweden an ideal case for analysing both the challenges and processes associated with democratic decision-making regarding location of public services.

Outline of the Book

This book intends to introduce a framework for understanding and analysing location problems. In this introductory chapter, we have sketched the basic concepts and dimensions of the problem. In the following chapters, we intend to dive deeper into some of the discussions and illustrate how the problem unfolds at the practical level of local governments.

Chapter 2 outlines the main conflicts of interest and the clashes that render location of public services a difficult and contentious matter, specifically focusing on the centre-periphery divide and the complex interests of citizens. The chapter also explores the public opinion on location issues using data from Swedish surveys.

Chapter 3 discusses location decisions from a legitimacy perspective and explains why legitimacy is crucial for long-term management of location. The chapter critically examines the concept of legitimacy, explores how legitimacy can be established or eroded, and discusses methods for evaluating legitimacy in this context.

Chapter 4 focuses on the institutional conditions of location in a multilevel government setting. It introduces the concept of multilevel governance (MLG) and examines its impact on varying conditions faced by local authorities. Additionally, this chapter delves into the significance of the size of sub-national entities and debates over the asymmetric allocation of responsibilities.

Chapter 5 explores the challenges of handling location issues in a representative democracy. It discusses the roles of parties and party conflicts, as well as the importance of policy congruence between voters and their elected representatives in locations issues.

Chapter 6 places the location dilemma in the politico-administrative system. It introduces the democratic ideals of antagonism and consensus, and critically discusses methods and consequences of public influence and participation in decision-making.

Chapter 7 focuses on how location problems can be solved. We suggest and discuss some broad learnings for practical management and end by providing some suggestions for future research.

References

Agnew, J. A. (1987). *Place and politics: The geographical mediation of state and society*. Routledge.

Aldrich, D. P. (2016). *Site fights: Divisive facilities and civil society in Japan and the West*. Cornell University Press.

Been, V. (1992). What's fairness got to do with it? Environmental justice and the siting of locally undesirable land uses. *Cornell Law Review, 78*, 1001.

Carson, D. B., Carson, D. A., Lundmark, L., & Hurtig, A. K. (2022). Resource deserts, village hierarchies and degrowth in sparsely populated areas: The case of Southern Lapland, Sweden. *Fennia, 200*(2), 210–227.

Cedering, M., & Wihlborg, E. (2020). Village schools as a hub in the community – A time-geographical analysis of the closing of two rural schools in southern Sweden. *Journal of Rural Studies, 80*, 606–617.

Christiaanse, S., & Haartsen, T. (2017). The influence of symbolic and emotional meaning of rural facilities on reactions to closure: The case of the village supermarket. *Journal of Rural Studies, 54,* 326–336.
de Fine Licht, J., Karlsson, D., & Skoog, L. (2023). Här, där eller överallt? Medborgares åsikter om lokalisering av offentlig service. In U. Andersson, P. Öhberg, A. Carlander, J. Martinsson, & N. Thorin (Eds.), *Ovisshetens tid.* The SOM-Institute, University of Gothenburg.
Dear, M. (1992). Understanding and overcoming the NIMBY syndrome. *Journal of the American Planning Association, 58*(3), 288–300.
Eriksson, E. (2023, November 13). Kan inte lova att vi öppnar i januari. *Folkbladet Västerbotten.*
Erlingsson, G. Ó., Öhrvall, R., Wallman Lundåsen, S., & Zerne, A. (2021). *Centrum mot periferi?: Om missnöje och framtidstro i Sveriges olika landsdelar* (version 2). Linköping University Electronic Press.
Erlingsson, G., Karlsson, D., Wide, J., & Öhrvall, R. (2022). *Demokratirådets rapport 2022: Den lokala demokratins vägval.* SNS.
Fredriksson, M., & Moberg, L. (2018). Costs will rather increase: Actions and arguments against decommissioning in local health services in Sweden. *Journal of Health Organization and Management, 32*(8), 943–961.
Gilljam, M., & Karlsson, D. (2015). Ruling majority and opposition: How parliamentary position affects the attitudes of political representatives. *Parliamentary Affairs, 68*(3), 555–572.
Greenberg, M. (1993). Proving environmental inequity in siting locally unwanted land uses. *Risk, 4,* 235.
Grimes, M., & Esaiasson, P. (2014). Government responsiveness: A democratic value with negative externalities? *Political Research Quarterly, 67*(4), 758–768.
Hawthorne, T. L., & Kwan, M.-P. (2012). Using GIS and perceived distance to understand the unequal geographies of healthcare in lower-income urban neighborhoods. *The Geographical Journal, 178*(1), 18–30.
Hodgart, R. L. (1978). Optimizing access to public services: A review of problems, models and methods of locating central facilities. *Progress in Human Geography, 2*(1), 17–48.
Hunold, C., & Young, I. M. (1998). Justice, democracy, and hazardous siting. *Political Studies, XLVI,* 82–95.
Kantur, E. (2024). *På spaning efter de bibliotek som flytt. En rapport om folkbibliotek ur ett lokaliseringsperspektiv.* School of Public Administration, University of Gothenburg.
Karlsson, D., & Skoog, L. (2023). *Lokalisering av offentlig service som politikområde – partipolitiska åsiktskonflikter i svenska kommuner.* School of Public Administration Working Paper Series 36. University of Gothenburg.
Kejerhag, J. (2023, January 23). Lycksele BB stängt – höggravida Emma tvingas köra 30 mil. *Dagens Nyheter.*
Ladner, A., Keuffer, N., & Baldersheim, H. (2016). Measuring local autonomy in 39 countries (1990–2014). *Regional and Federal Studies, 26*(3), 321–357.

Larsson Taghizadeh, J. (2016). *Power from below?: The impact of protests and lobbying on school closures in Sweden.* Doctoral dissertation, Uppsala University.

Lasswell, H. D. (1936). *Politics: Who gets what, when, how.* Whittlesey House.

Lidström, A. (2015). Swedish local and regional government in a European context. In J. Pierre (Ed.), *The Oxford handbook of Swedish politics.* Oxford University Press.

Montin, S. (2015). Municipalities, regions, and county councils. In J. Pierre (Ed.), *The Oxford handbook of Swedish politics.* Oxford University Press.

Nabatchi, T., & Amsler, L. B. (2014). Direct public engagement in local government. *American Review of Public Administration, 44*(4S), 63S–88S.

Norris, P. (2022). *In praise of skepticism: Trust but verify.* Oxford University Press.

Österlind, H. (2023, January 13). Inlandsaktivisterna oroar sig för att stängning blir en norm. *Folkbladet Västerbotten.*

Pepermans, Y., & Loots, I. (2013). Wind farm struggles in Flanders fields: A sociological perspective. *Energy Policy, 59,* 321–328.

Pettersson, R. (2023, August 11). *Kommuner stöttar Åmåls fängelseplaner – samarbetet fördjupas.* Provinstidningen.

Pierson, P. (1996). The new politics of the welfare state. *World Politics, 48*(2), 143–179.

Pollitt, C. (2012). *New perspectives on public services: Place and technology.* Oxford University Press.

Proctor, R., & Simmons, S. (2000). Public library closures: The management of hard decisions. *Library Management, 21*(1), 25–34.

Sellers, J. M., Lidström, A., & Bae, Y. (2020). *Multilevel democracy: How local institutions and civil society shape the modern state.* Cambridge University Press.

Skoog, L. (2019). *Political conflicts: Dissent and antagonism among political parties in local government.* Doctoral dissertation, University of Gothenburg.

Skoog, L., & Svensson, P. (2023). Hidden policy conflicts? Administrative strategies to manage depoliticisation. *Acta Politica, 58*(4), 819–836.

Starke, P. (2006). The politics of welfare state retrenchment: A literature review. *Social Policy and Administration, 40*(1), 104–120.

Stewart, E., & Aitken, M. (2015). Beyond NIMBYs and NOOMBYs: What can wind farm controversies teach us about public involvement in hospital closures? *BMC Health Services Research, 15,* 1–6.

Strandh, V. (2023). *Hur kan service och trygghetspunkter (SOT) på landsbygden stärka lokalsamhällens krisberedskap och förmåga att hantera kriser?* Umeå Working Papers in Crisis Management Studies.

Syssner, J. (2020). *Pathways to demographic adaptation: Perspectives on policy and planning in depopulating areas in Northern Europe.* Springer Nature.

Törnwall, M. (2023, March 2). Ökat stöd för danska vindkraftverk. *Svenska Dagbladet.*

Tyler, T. R. (2006). Psychological perspectives on legitimacy and legitimation. *Annual Review of Psychology, 57,* 375–400.

Wolf, E. A., & Van Dooren, W. (2018). Conflict reconsidered: The boomerang effect of depolitization in the policy process. *Public Administration, 96,* 286–301.

CHAPTER 2

The Centre-Periphery Divide

The physical placement of a service facility, as well as the spatial allocation (e.g. Fredriksson, 2017) of a number of facilities within a polity more generally, is important for citizens as the geographical proximity determines their accessibility to these services. This spatial allocation of service facilities, and its degree of centralisation and decentralisation within and between territories, is vital for understanding the inherent conflict of interests in the *centre-periphery divide*, as people in the periphery normally have longer to travel than others. Applying a centre–periphery perspective on the location of services highlights how geographical areas are in an asymmetric power dynamic with each other, where the centre is often favoured and the periphery frequently disadvantaged in terms of both the distribution of influence over decision-making processes and access to public services. In this chapter, we will unpack this perspective and explore how these conflicting interests are articulated in the context of determining the spatial allocation of services, and the centralisation and decentralisation of service facilities, in relation to values such as accessibility, efficiency, and quality.

However, what makes this perspective so multifaceted is the often elusive and relative nature of whether groups of individuals reside in the centre or the periphery. Moreover, the same group, or even an individual, may harbour several different interests concurrently—pertaining to the very same locational issue—depending on whether they perceive themselves as a service user based in a particular geographical location or a citizen and member of a wider community.

The conflicts of interest inherent in this policy area make it challenging from a democratic standpoint to find legitimate solutions and make legitimate decisions. The second part of this chapter will delve into the question of public opinion on locational issues, with arguments illustrated by results from a citizen survey conducted in Sweden in 2022.

What Do We Mean with the Centre-Periphery Divide?

The interest for territorial inequality and political geography has had an upswing in recent years as there is growing concerns among democracy scholars worldwide regarding escalating tensions between central and peripheral areas.

The centre and periphery dichotomy has been used in the social science literature for a long time, and researchers have, as we shall see, attached different meanings to this concept. In this book, we start from the basic idea that underlies most of the previous research: in a polity—be it a country, a region, or a municipality—there often exists a tension or conflict of interests between favoured and disadvantaged geographical areas. This conflict is here referred to as the centre-periphery divide. Places with significant political and economic influence are referred to as centres, while less influential and less resourceful geographical areas are referred to as peripheries. Political decisions are often made in centres, and these decisions generally have substantial implications for the periphery.

The centre-periphery divide becomes particularly relevant every time a political decision is made that has a geographical dimension implying that not all parts of a polity are treated equally. In such instances, decisions can often be perceived as favouring or disadvantaging specific locales and their inhabitants (cf., Munis, 2022). The planning and location of public services stand as prime examples of such decisions. The balance between centre and periphery may differ across polities due to the relative prominence of the centre in comparison to the periphery—within countries or within municipalities. Perhaps contra-intuitively, it is when the periphery is relatively strong that the centre-periphery divide translates into heightened political conflict, and when the centre is dominant the periphery is less able to push back—conflicts are lowered (Skoog & Karlsson, 2018). But when patterns of resentment and antagonism become entrenched and manifest across diverse situations and issues, the divide is established.

What further complicates this issue is that what constitutes as a centre and a periphery can shift based on our perspective. A small town might function as a dominant centre in relation to its rural surroundings but appear distinctly peripheral when contrasted with a larger regional city. This larger city, in turn, might be peripheral when compared to the nation's capital. Such dynamics is very evident in location of public services. This means that the centre-periphery divide transcends a simplified urban-rural dichotomy and can also be found between, for example, more and less resourceful parts of the same city or municipality.

One way to understand the foundation of the centre-periphery divide is to view it as a societal cleavage structure. Cleavage theory and the concepts of centre-periphery have strong ties to the works of Lipset and Rokkan (Lipset & Rokkan, 1967; Rokkan, 1970), who argued that the present-day party systems are entwined with decisions made and alliances forged in the past. Throughout the nation-building processes, cleavages emerged from the power dynamics between central authorities and the national government often pitted against local and regional actors. These divisions, which often were rooted in territorial conflicts, still influence politics and political behaviour. Based on their work, two historical cleavages stand out as particularly relevant for understanding centre and periphery. The first refers to suppressed ethnical, linguistic, and religious minorities who often resided in peripheries and their resistance towards a nation-building elite. The second refers to the relation between rural property-owners and growing bourgeoisie in urban centres (Lipset & Rokkan, 1967; Saglie et al., 2020). These cleavages both have territory and geography at its core. And historical developments relating to these cleavages have left a lasting mark on the contemporary political arena, shaping the dynamics of power, alliances, and ideological orientations.

However, while much research on dynamics between centres and peripheries—or urban and rural areas—often may be sprung from Lipset and Rokkan's advancement of the idea of oppositional poles between places, researchers now often associate many more factors into the concept centre and periphery (Saglie, 2023, p. 278). Among more recent labels that illustrate such dynamics between geographic areas, we find 'places that matter' and 'places that don't matter' (Rodríguez-Pose, 2018), where the underlying argument is that big cities are the engine for creating economic growth, making them matter more than less densely populated spaces with less potential for growth or perhaps even a declining local economy. Concurrently, there is a movement where places that are 'lagging-behind' are starting to revolt via the ballot-box, leading to a surge in support for populistic alternatives in rural areas (Huijsmans, 2023; Rickardsson, 2021), giving rise to debates on so-called geographies of discontent (Dijkstra et al., 2020; McCann, 2020). Citizens in peripheries are also more prone to have a negative view of the capital city (Rickardsson et al., 2021), exhibit lower trust in political representatives (Stein et al., 2021). Research has also shown that 'public service wastelands'—areas with a long-term lack of public services—will spur geographic discontent (Stroppe, 2023) and increase support for the far right (Cremaschi et al., 2023; Wallman Lundåsen, 2024).

A bottom-up perspective, where focus is placed on the viewpoint of citizens, has in recent years added new nuances to these debates (Eidheim & Fimreite, 2020, p. 60). This is rooted in the notion that shared economic and symbolic grievances may reinforce a sense of community among individuals who share geographical identity. Cramer (2012, 2016) launched the concept 'rural consciousness', which refers to the idea that the place where an individual resides can shape the identity of that person—influencing how individuals process political information. Some of the characteristics incorporated into a rural consciousness are: a sense that rural and urban residents have different values and lifestyles; that urban residents neither understands nor respects rural residents; the view that rural areas are unfairly treated and are ignored by policymakers; or that a belief that rural districts do not get their share of public resources (Cramer, 2012). Other scholars contend that this sentiment extends beyond the centre-periphery divide, finding expression even within urban territories, for example in suburbs or districts feeling marginalised relative to urban centres (Crulli, 2022). Munis (2022) argues that the broader concept 'place-based resentment' is more suitable, as frustration and feelings of being short-changed are felt not only by rural residents. Troublingly, perceived absence of communal solidarity could compromise the consensus required for implementing collective solutions to societal challenges. Under such conditions, legitimising political decisions concerning the location of services becomes exceedingly challenging. In sum, these debates show that power dynamics between geographical places has important implications for citizens' perspectives on location of public services and infrastructures.

Although the centre-periphery divide is intrinsic to most political systems, place-based resentment can be mitigated. A principal objective in this regard must be to forestall this predicament by organising society in a manner that garners acceptance—if not always approval—from both central and peripheral populations. One key area that this applies to is decisions on centralisation and decentralisation of services.

CENTRALISATION AND DECENTRALISATION OF PUBLIC SERVICE FACILITIES

The *spatial allocation* of public service facilities, that is the distribution of service facilities over a particular geographical area, as well as the centralisation or decentralisation of facilities in relation to local centres and peripheries, is key issues in most location decisions. These issues are relevant in all contexts where citizens' lives spread out over a geographical area, which is to say, virtually everywhere. In cities, it may concern which suburbs should have services (c.f. Soja, 2013), while in rural areas it could be about which locations beside the main town should maintain services. From a national standpoint, the issue involves deciding where state administration should be located and promoting a policy ensuring equal conditions throughout the country (Marshall, 2007).

Discussions on spatial allocations of services, as well as on the division of responsibilities for public services within and between tiers of government, have been ongoing for a long time (e.g. Hutchcroft, 2001). The challenge and controversy arise from the need to balance cost-effective and high-quality operations with ensuring service accessibility to everyone, irrespective of their residence. The problem is that achieving efficiency and quality can be challenging when services are allocated to many small, dispersed units. Through economies of scale, it is possible to save on administrative costs and make the best use of personnel with specialised skills. While such gains may be attainable (e.g. Giancotti et al., 2017), these are often difficult to measure in many public operations. Closely linked to the issue of economies of scale is the question of skill provision. Even if there is sufficient demand to justify a service unit, it cannot function without qualified staff. In rural peripheries, staffing is one of the biggest challenges (Jones et al., 2019; Vaughan et al., 2018). The staffing challenge in rural areas is shared with the private sector (de Hoyos & Green, 2011) and cannot easily be resolved by merely increasing financial allocations. Concentrating services to larger units in the centre may be the only viable option for keeping key personnel.

Opponents of centralising service facilities to local centres often question the validity of arguments favouring service concentration, which are typically case-specific and difficult to measure. However, the primary argument for decentralisation of facilities to achieve increased service proximity primarily concerns the value of maintaining equal access to services in the country as a whole. Centralising services into larger units in the centre would require individuals in peripheral areas to travel greater distances to access these services (Syed et al., 2013), consequently reducing their ability to remain in their local communities. And for certain issues, having longer distances can be a serious health hazard or even a life-threatening risk (e.g. Grzybowski et al., 2011; Avdic, 2016). Moreover, the capacity to travel varies among individuals, influenced by factors such as physical mobility and financial resources. Consequently, if centralisation results in decreased service accessibility, it could exacerbate inequality among citizens. The term spatial equity is often used for describing the degree of fairness in the spatial allocation of public services, although there is no consensus on how it should be measured (e.g. Whitehead et al., 2019).

In summary, deciding on service locations often requires a difficult political balancing act. It involves aligning the interests of citizens in both central and peripheral areas, as well as considering the needs of the entire population.

The Interests of Service Users and Citizens

While the centre-periphery divide highlights conflicts between central and peripheral populations regarding the spatial allocation of services, there exists another significant division in interests concerning decisions about service location. This distinction is between those who are users of a particular service and those who are not. The self-interest of service users is naturally related to the quality of the service and their access to it. From a location perspective, the proximity of the service is crucial, enabling convenient use and minimising the time and costs for users travelling to distant service locations.

Non-users, however, may have limited interest in keeping up the quality of services they do not use and even less in paying the higher taxes needed to keep others' access to these services at a high level. Yet, this narrow self-interest perspective might broaden when considering that non-users today could be future users or that they may have relatives or friends who are users. Consequently, they might still have an interest in ensuring the quality and availability of these services for when they or their loved ones need them.

However, both non-users and users may share a vested interest in the prosperity and benefits of their locality, as both groups are citizens in a broader sense—members and taxpayers of their local community. Availability of services in a locality enhances its attractiveness, bolsters its competitive edge in attracting jobs, business growth, tourism, and perhaps even drawing in new residents. For example, even if an individual does not have children and is not directly impacted by having a school nearby, they may still value its presence for the overall attractiveness and future prosperity of their local community. However, as taxpayers, they may also be concerned about the efficient use of public funds and strive to avoid costly location solutions that could diminish resources for other essential services or result in unreasonably high taxes.

The roles of non-users and service users are interconnected, resulting in multiple self- and collective interests that may conflict with each other, with no clear resolution in sight. What is perceived as most important can vary from individual to individual, but also more broadly. With the introduction of marketisation solutions in the public sector, the role of the user—or customer—has been emphasised, and the individual perspective has gained predominance over the collective (Aberbach & Christensen, 2005). From an analytical perspective, however, it is still useful to distinguish the different values associated with various roles/interests in order to clarify the existing contradictions. As illustrated in Fig. 2.1, from the narrow self-interest of service users, quality and proximity are two key

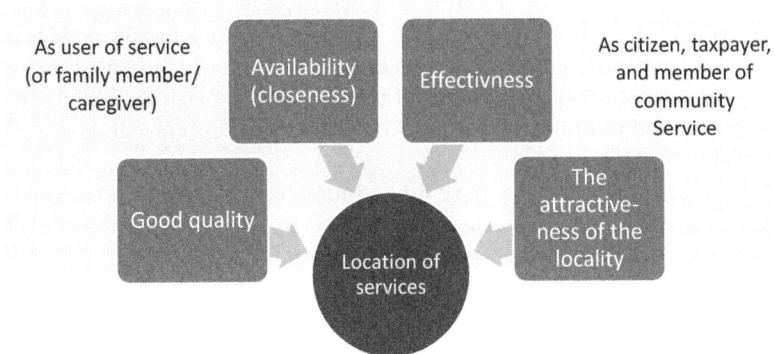

Fig. 2.1 Local citizen interest in relation location of public services

values affected by location decisions, whereas for non-users, their primary interests lie in assessing the efficiency of public operations and valuing the local area's prosperity and attractiveness as community members.

This depiction in Fig. 2.1 of four values relating to citizen interests in this manner is, of course, a simplification of a complex situation especially as each value is often difficult to define and is relative to the circumstances. The *accessibility and proximity* to services, for example, is an aspect of approaching location problems that might seem straightforward to unravel, almost in a scientific manner. The distance from a person's home to a service facility can be measured—both in terms of physical distance and in the amount of time it takes to travel using available means of transport (there is a whole field of spatial allocation/equity research concerned with such efforts, e.g. Fredriksson, 2017). Yet, distance is also a social construct, where perceptions of what is near or far are shaped by habits and expectations (de Fine Licht et al., 2023). In urban areas, a service facility in a different district may feel distant, whereas the same distance in a rural community might be considered just around the corner. Individuals' time perceptions also vary; for a time-pressed working parent, every additional minute spent ferrying children to various schools and activities is precious, whereas for a retired individual in a rural setting, the journey to a health centre might constitute an enjoyable day out. For emergency services or transporting critically ill patients to hospital, distances can be a matter of life or death, with significant risks associated with delays (Avdic, 2016).

Assessing the quality of public services is no less complex. Even with satisfaction surveys and performance reviews giving insights into operational effectiveness, there are many aspects to consider that are abstract and difficult to quantify. Educational quality, for example, involves more than just test scores and grades; it includes the working environment and the safety of both children and personnel (e.g. Kutsyuruba et al., 2015). Challenges faced by small rural schools often include teaching pupils of varying ages in the same classroom, placing significant demands and responsibility on teachers who frequently work alone (Raggl, 2015). However, establishing positive social networks for children is arguably easier in small, rural schools, which are closer to their homes. In healthcare, a qualified local doctor may suffice for standard cases, but for patients with unusual symptoms, specialist care at larger, centralised facilities is often preferable. This ensures that the physicians have adequate experience with similar cases. The quality of care also encompasses resilience in situations where staff shortages or illnesses occur, making rapid solutions challenging in rural schools or healthcare centres (e.g. Vaughan et al., 2018). Simultaneously, the impersonal nature and bureaucratic logistics inherent in large-scale education and healthcare systems can detract from the quality of service experienced.

As a citizen and taxpayer, the individual has a vested interest in ensuring that their hard-earned money, paid in taxes, is utilised in the best possible manner and allocated between essential purposes in a reasonable and equitable fashion. The concern is not the promotion of a single service but the functionality of the system as a whole. Allocating extra resources to enhance the quality and accessibility of a specific service becomes problematic if these resources are diverted from other areas of equal or greater importance. Thus, using public funds as efficiently as possible is a central political value and of personal interest for taxpayers who otherwise face the risk of increased taxes. The challenge, of course, lies in the fact that it is often difficult to determine which solution is the most effective, and it is not always easy to balance short-term savings against long-term effects. Studies suggest that even laypeople can have a good overall understanding of the state of the municipal economy (Donatella & Karlsson, 2023), but it is a lot to ask of them that they should have a deep understanding of financial intricacies.

Fighting for LALUs: School Closures in Sweden

'Why should children be forced to ride the bus for several hours every day to school?' The headline of the opinion piece in a local newspaper provides a powerful illustration of how the village school has come to symbolise the centre-periphery divide in Sweden. While centralisation to fewer units also is a trend in cities, the debate on small rural schools is often particularly heated. The village school offers more than just education; it is often a pivotal community hub, one of the few employers for highly educated in the area, and a symbol for the vitality and prospective future of the location (Autti & Hyry-Beihammer, 2014; Cedering & Wihlborg, 2020).

School closures are one of the main sources of local conflicts in the Nordic countries (e.g. Larsson Taghizadeh, 2016; Uba, 2016; Strandberg & Berg, 2019; Isaksson, 2023) and elsewhere (e.g. Kearns et al., 2009; Tieken & Auldridge-Reveles, 2019). In a survey where local politicians in Sweden were asked in a free-text format what they saw as the hardest decision to make as a representative, 26 per cent mentioned school closures (de Fine Licht & Esaiasson, 2023). Proposals, or even vague rumours about potential proposals, to close schools are often met with heavy criticism, to the extent that local politicians often hesitate to even suggest a closure unless there is little to no doubt of the necessity to do so.

At the same time, the number of closed schools have increased in Sweden (Uba, 2016; Fogelholm et al., 2019), and as elementary schools are a municipal responsibility in Sweden, many local representatives will at some point meet angry parents, disappointed teachers, and a local community fighting for its survival. Decision-makers are trapped in a web of conflicting considerations about quality assurance, economic efficiency, legal demands, recruiting qualified personnel, and public opinion. The overarching question is: how much should the population as a whole be expected to sacrifice for the well-being of a smaller group? And to what extent should someone choosing to live in remote and peripheral areas be expected to fend for themselves?

The fourth type of citizen interest involves values that are not based on direct outcomes for the individual but rather on the well-being of the society they live in. This includes a desire for prosperity and a promising future of one's local community, akin to wishing well for one's family members. Many people have strong connections to their place of origin—be it a village, city, or region. These connections are a part of their identity and their social relationships and often shape a deep-seated interest in the welfare of their local area. Such collective interests relate to the concept of 'sociotropic concerns'—that is concerns for a social collective (Kiewiet & Lewis-Beck, 2011; Kinder & Kiewiet, 1981; Meehl, 1977), which has been used to refer to place-based concerns for a specific geographical community (Wallman Lundåsen & Erlingsson, 2023). As sociotropic concerns influence people's political perceptions, their priorities revolve around the welfare of their local community, not just their own personal interests. Instead of being driven by self-interest (*ego*tropic concerns), these stances are shaped by desires to enhance the quality of life for all residents in their local community, regardless of how these changes might personally affect them.

The presence of a public service facility, from this latter perspective, can signify much more than the utility of the service it provides; it can represent an expression of community and territorial identity. Proposals to close facilities can be seen as a death knell for the community, a threat that impacts and distresses all those who are invested in seeing their hometown thrive.

This highlights the challenge of categorising citizens based on their interests in a location decision. Individuals may hold multiple interests simultaneously, influenced by whether they reside in the centre or periphery, and whether they are users of the service in question, and the extent to which they value the overall well-being of the community. The interplay between individual and collective interests in location issues raises the question of how people's political opinions on these matters are formed, and what the general public opinion is. Understanding this complexity is crucial in assessing the dynamics of community-based decision-making and policy development.

Public Opinion on Location Issues

In a democratic society where policies are expected to align with the will of the people, the study of public opinion is particularly important, especially in location issues where individual and collective interests are so complex. To illustrate how opinions on location issues can be examined and what factors influence them, we have the opportunity to present some findings from a Swedish citizen survey, the National SOM Survey 2022, where we have posed a number of questions on this theme. The Society, Opinon & Media (SOM) surveys are conducted by means of postal questionnaires sent to randomly selected people aged 16–85 living in Sweden (Bergquist et al., 2023). Our questions were answered by over 1600 people. (A more detailed description of these results in Swedish can be found in de Fine Licht et al., 2023.)

To understand the fundamental or ideological reasoning behind citizens' views on the location of public services from a spatial allocation point of view, we developed a survey question that captures the key ideological trade-off between centralisation and decentralisation. We asked respondents to consider the primary values associated with both concepts and to place themselves on a scale from 0 to 10, indicating their preference for either, or neither, of these opposing positions (referred to hereafter as the c/d-scale). Details of the question's wording and its results are presented in Fig. 2.2, along with the distribution of answers. This question has also been posed to elected representatives at all levels of government in Sweden (Karlsson, 2022). In Chap. 5, we will explore how well political parties and politicians reflect public opinion on this matter.

The results in Fig. 2.2 show that citizens' opinions are spread across the entire c/d-scale—from extreme centralisers to extreme decentralisers. However, in Swedish public opinion there is a clear predominance of individuals leaning towards decentralisation (43 per cent compared to 25 per cent favouring centralisation). The single most common response alternative, however, was the neutral middle option (32 per cent), which likely indicates that the question is difficult to answer and a reluctance to clearly favour one side over the other.

In addition to this principled question we formulated additional survey questions in the form of six proposals relating to the location of specific services or infrastructure facilities: 'to preserve primary schools in rural/less populated areas'; 'to introduce financial support for grocery stores in rural areas'; 'to centralise specialist healthcare in major hospitals' and 'to centralise research and higher education at major universities'; as well as

When it comes to the location of services, there is somtimes talk of a political dimension between:

1) Those who want centralised public services (for the sake of efficiency and quality).
2) Those who want decentralised public services (to promote equitable access to services everywhere).

Where would you place yourself on the following scale?

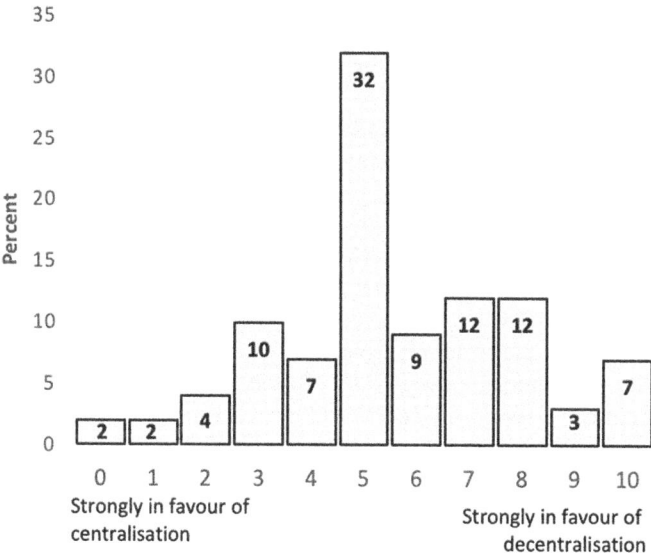

Fig. 2.2 Public opinion in Sweden 2022 on the ideological trade-off between centralisation and decentralisation of public services (the c/d-scale), per cent. (Source: The National SOM Survey 2022, $N = 1674$. *Note*: The figure illustrates the distribution of opinions among Swedish individuals regarding the survey question referenced in the figure)

'to build more wind turbines in my municipality' and 'to invest in high-speed train connections between major cities'.

These proposals were designed to capture various types of activities and responsibilities across different tiers of government in Sweden. The proposal to provide financial support to grocery stores in rural areas is notable as this has not traditionally been considered a public concern. However, it significantly influences where people can live, leading to potential public financial support for rural stores. The establishment of wind turbines involves both positive municipal attitudes (which have planning monopoly and veto power) for private wind power installation and the municipality's role as an energy producer building the power plants themselves. Other questions concerning education, healthcare, higher education, and railways are more traditionally public concerns, although there is debate over the extent to which market forces should influence service location and distribution necessary for national viability. Four of the proposals relate to public services, while two concern public policy for establishing services and public goods that could also be private (supporting grocery stores and building wind turbines).

Two of the proposals are clearly decentralist (preserving schools and supporting grocery stores), while two are centralist (centralising specialist healthcare and higher education). Building wind turbines in municipalities is fundamentally a decentralist proposal, while high-speed train tracks between major cities favour centralism. The question of establishing wind turbines can encompass a positive stance from municipalities (with planning monopoly and veto) for the establishment of private wind power, as well as the municipality acting as an energy producer to build power turbines. The other questions regarding schools, healthcare, and higher education are more classic public concerns, even though there is also a debate about how much market forces should be allowed to influence where services are available and how widespread they need to be for the whole country to thrive. The results from these questions are presented in Fig. 2.3.

Despite the proposals covering diverse issues, involving both decentralisation and centralisation, all were favoured by a plurality of respondents. The most popular of the six proposals are of a decentralist nature, with 88 per cent positively viewing 'preserving schools in rural/less populated areas' and 70 per cent agreeing that 'introducing financial support for grocery stores in rural areas' is a good proposal. Only 2 and 8 per cent, respectively, viewed these as bad proposals. It is noteworthy that a political proposal involving difficult priorities, such as the issue of schools in rural areas, has such overwhelming support in public opinion. A majority, 54 per cent, support 'building more wind turbines in [their] municipality', though this issue also has a relatively high proportion of explicitly negative views (21 per cent).

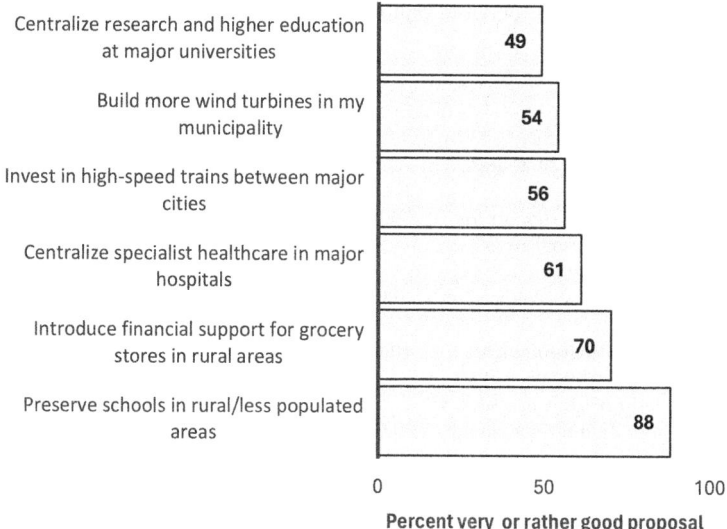

Fig. 2.3 Support for political proposals regarding location issues (per cent). (Source: The national SOM survey 2022, N = 1707–1738. *Note*: The question was, 'What is your opinion on the following proposals?', and the responses were given on a five-graded scale from very good to very bad proposal. The figure illustrates the percentage who responded very good or rather good proposal. The proposals are sorted according to popularity, with the least popular proposals first)

However, centralist proposals also find support: 61 per cent are positive about 'centralising specialist healthcare in major hospitals', 56 per cent favour 'investing in high-speed trains between major cities', and 49 per cent think that 'centralising research and higher education at major universities' is a good idea (with 17–22 per cent opposing).

A correlation analysis (Table 2.1) indicates that opinions on the two explicitly decentralist proposals regarding schools and grocery stores are relatively strongly correlated ($r = +0.36$). This is not surprising since both are aimed at supporting those living in sparsely populated areas. Similarly, opinions on the two explicit centralist proposals (pertaining to hospitals and universities) are also strongly interrelated ($r = +0.39$), as both involve activities requiring high specialist expertise and are proposed for centralisation. The third distinct relationship between issues is that between the establishment of wind power and high-speed trains ($r = +0.30$), likely

Table 2.1 Correlation between pinions on different service location proposals (Pearson's r)

	(1)	(2)	(3)	(4)	(5)
Proposals of decentralisation					
• Preserve schools in rural/less populated areas	–				
• Introduce financial support for grocery stores in rural areas	+0.36***	–			
Proposals of centralisation					
• Centralise specialist healthcare in major hospitals	−0.01	+0.05**	–		
• Centralise research and higher education at major universities	+0.03	+0.09***	0.39***	–	
Proposal of infrastructure development					
• Build more wind turbines in my municipality	−0.04	+0.03	+0.01	+0.01	–
• Invest in high-speed trains between major cities	−0.02	−0.04*	−0.00	−0.01	+0.30***

Source: The national SOM survey 2022, N = 1707–1738

Note: The formulation of the questions and response alternatives are described in Table 1

***$p < 0.01$, **$p < 0.05$, *$p < 0.1$

connected by their focus on infrastructure and environmental aspects, and the ambition to decrease fossil fuel dependency through technological investments.

The most notable observation from the correlation analyses in Table 2.1 is the absence of correlations between opinions on most issues. There are no substantial negative correlations between views on centralisation and decentralisation proposals, as would be expected if individuals were consistently decentralist or centralist. Surprisingly, there are even slight positive correlations between support for grocery stores in rural areas and advocating the centralisation of hospitals and universities. A reasonable interpretation of these findings is that most people do not see these issues as part of the same centralisation–decentralisation continuum of service. Different considerations are made for different types of policies—and being positive about centralisation in one area does not mean being negative about decentralisation in another. And as the first part of this chapter indicated, the conflicts of interests for individuals and groups are multi-layered.

To understand the potential factors influencing individuals' opinions on the location of services, we employed regression analyses across several models not presented in this chapter due to space constraints (see de Fine Licht et al., 2023). These models included explanatory factors that capture background characteristics such as age, gender, family status, level of education, income, origin, religiosity, and interpersonal trust. Additionally, we included residential locations, categorised into rural and metropolitan municipalities. The models also take into account individuals' proximity to the nearest service point for various services. For ideological factors, we used self-placement on the left-right political spectrum and people's principled views on location issues, as indicated by the c/d-scale mentioned above.

A first key observation from these analyses is the impact of residence on opinion: individuals residing in rural areas tend to be more decentralist on the c/d-scale and are somewhat more inclined to financially support grocery stores in rural areas. This could be seen as an expected manifestation of their self-interest. Both these findings suggest that people's interests play a role in shaping public opinion on location issues. Nonetheless, one of the most surprising discoveries is the relative weakness of geographical explanations for people's opinions, beyond these two notable exceptions. A crucial outcome of the analysis is that perceived proximity to services has almost no significance in explaining opinions on location proposals. The individual factor, which at first glance seemed a clear indicator of self-interest in location issues, is in fact almost negligible in several of the survey questions.

Unfortunately, we do not have the capacity to determine whether respondents are themselves users of the services mentioned in the question, with one exception: we can examine whether the presence of children in respondents' homes influence people's opinions on schools in rural areas. The answer is that it does not. Additionally, there is no interaction effect suggesting that parents of young children in rural areas are more eager than others to support proposals regarding preserving rural schools.

If self-interest, related to residential location or service usage, does not straightforwardly shape opinions, might people instead be more influenced by principled and ideological positions when forming their views on service location? Indeed, the findings suggest that ideological/principled stances do have an explanatory role, though it is limited. The position on the c/d-scale (used here as an independent variable) shows relatively strong negative impacts on attitudes towards centralisation proposals for hospitals and universities, and a positive, albeit weak, effect on decentralisation proposals for schools. Regarding grocery stores, there are no notable effects linked to the c/d-scale. It is also worth noting the modest ideological effects of left-right positioning: those on the political right tend to favour university centralisation and are less inclined to support financial aid for rural grocery stores. Additionally, views on wind turbines and train services align with the left-right spectrum, where right-leaning individuals are more opposed to these proposals.

In relative terms, ideological factors contribute more to explanatory power than indicators intended to capture people's interests related to their place of residence. However, ideological connections in these matters are weaker than in other types of political issues such as those more closely aligned with the left-right spectrum or the GAL-TAN (Green-Alternative Libertarian vs. Traditional-Authoritarian) dimension. Nevertheless, a significant portion of the variation in people's views remains unexplained. How people position themself regarding proposals on service location cannot be easily explained by self-interest in terms of perceived service proximity, nor purely by ideological or principled stances.

When interpreting public opinion from all these angles, it would be erroneous to conclude that interest and ideology are irrelevant in location issues. That is not the case. What we can assert is that location issues within public opinion do not represent a one-dimensional political aspect that can be explained by easily identifiable interests and ideological positions. Instead, our interpretation is that conflicts of interest and principled value conflicts are indeed prevalent in this policy area and have discernible effects on certain issues, but they are likely far more complex than what simple survey tools typically used in public opinion research can capture.

One aspect that lends credibility to this conclusion is the numerous and extensive political disputes ongoing in Swedish municipalities on these matters, where citizens actively engage on various fronts—most notably in opposition to the centralisation of services. Such protest activities would not arise if there were not deeply felt interests perceived as being threatened.

To Eat One's Cake and Have It Too

The discussion regarding the location of public services and its relation to the centre-periphery divide has not only highlighted the conflicts of interest between individuals and between geographically defined groups but

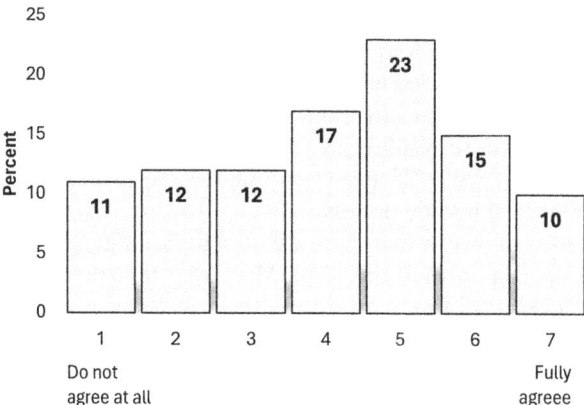

Fig. 2.4 Those who choose to live in rural areas/smaller localities must be prepared for poorer access to services (per cent). (Source: The National SOM Survey 2022. *Note*: The question reads: 'To what extent do you agree that those who choose to live in rural areas/smaller localities must be prepared for poorer access to services?' and responses are indicated on a scale from 1 'Do not agree at all' to 7 'Fully agree'. $N = 1734$)

has also exposed a general reluctance to prioritise between these conflicting values. Support for a decentralised service organisation is widespread, especially relating to schools, among both rural and urban populations. The lack of strong correlations between opinions and where people reside shows that opinion is formed not primarily by narrow self-interest but rather by societal values and collective interests that consider what is best for the local community—and likely a genuine solidarity with rural populations among those who, even if not personally benefiting, wish for rural areas to thrive.

However, this reluctance to prioritise is problematic from a democratic perspective. In a world of limited resources—particularly in rural areas facing pessimism due to urbanisation and economic restructuring—the location of services close to citizens in the periphery is costly, and these expenses may necessitate prioritisation in relation to other significant political goals. In a survey directed at citizens, we sought to gauge public awareness of this dilemma. We framed the question as a statement, asking respondents to consider that those who choose to live in rural areas or smaller localities must be prepared for poorer access to services. The results are presented in Fig. 2.4.

As observed in Fig. 2.4, there is a broad range of opinions, with a relatively high number of respondents aligning themselves at the extreme ends of the scale. This clearly illustrates the divisive nature of the issue. The general trend indicates that almost half (48 per cent) of the respondents agree that those residing in rural areas must be prepared for less accessible services, while 35 per cent disagree. Seventeen per cent have selected the neutral middle option.

Further analysis reveals that there are no significant geographical factors influencing the responses to this issue. Moreover, the correlation between individuals' answers to this question and their opinions on decentralisation and centralisation measured by the c/d-scale (see Fig. 2.2) is surprisingly weak ($r = -0.14$), where those with a tendency towards the centralist position on the c/d-scale are slightly more likely to agree with the statement. The overriding impression, however, is that people do not necessarily equate the decentralisation of services with the provision of equal access to services for all, irrespective of their location.

This presentation of public opinion on location issues in Sweden indicates that responses provided by citizens at times are contradictory and may have varying motives. Even though there seems to be a widespread preference for decentralisation of services and facilities across both rural and urban communities, real-world politics means that as there are limited resources prioritisations and difficult decisions must be made. Troublingly, we saw that general public opinion may not always provide decision-makers with a map to follow when resources are constrained. Returning to the centre-periphery divide and the risk of location decisions nurturing a 'place-based resentment', where residents of different geographical areas and those in other areas, it is of utmost importance that such decisions are made in a manner that citizens can accept. Thus, underscoring the challenges faced by decision-makers in a representative democracy in making location decisions that may, or may not, align with the will of both central and peripheral populations.

Summary

In this chapter, we have discussed the personal and collective interests of individuals and groups in relation to location of public services. The concept of a centre-periphery divide is built on the idea of oppositional poles between places and posit that if there are influential centres, there must also be less influential peripheries—and vice versa, where decisions made at the centre have significant impact for the periphery. Researchers have in recent years broadened perspectives on centre-periphery through the lens of 'rural consciousness' or a 'rural resentment', which is the idea that social and place-based identities in rural areas may be entwined with shared feelings of deprivation. Importantly, the idea of a 'place-based resentment' is the idea that these experiences extend beyond the periphery, encompassing the insight that all types of territories—rural as well as urban—may experience marginalisation and feelings of being short-changed. These power dynamics between places influence citizens' political perspectives in general and on public service locations in specific. The centre-periphery divide is of importance for understanding decisions with geographical dimensions, potentially seen as favouring or disadvantaging specific locales.

However, our analysis of survey data from Sweden of these conflicting interests indicates that the fact that people may have multiple self-interests in relation to specific location issues made it difficult to discern clear, unambiguous correlations between people's opinions on these issues and their assumed narrow self-interests. A connected complexity arises from shifting perspectives on what constitutes a centre and periphery, where a citizen might live in a central town in the municipality—but that this place might be peripheral in relation to the nation's capital city. It is this complexity that makes location issues so challenging to address—and even more difficult for decision-makers to find solutions that are perceived as legitimate by concerned citizens. Nevertheless, decisions must be made, and the question of legitimacy is critical. In the next chapter, we will delve deeper into how location issues can be understood from a legitimacy perspective.

References

Aberbach, J. D., & Christensen, T. (2005). Citizens and consumers. *Public Management Review, 7*(2), 225–246.

Autti, O., & Hyry-Beihammer, E. K. (2014). School closures in rural Finnish communities. *Journal of Research in Rural Education, 29*(1), 1–17.

Avdic, D. (2016). Improving efficiency or impairing access? Health care consolidation and quality of care: Evidence from emergency hospital closures in Sweden. *Journal of Health Economics, 48*, 44–60.

Bergquist, J., Falk, E., & Weissenbilder, M. (2023). *Den nationella SOM-undersökningen 2022 – En metodöversikt*. University of Gothenburg: The SOM Institute.

Cedering, M., & Wihlborg, E. (2020). Village schools as a hub in the community – A time-geographical analysis of the closing of two rural schools in southern Sweden. *Journal of Rural Studies, 80*, 606–617.

Cramer, K. J. (2012). Putting inequality in its place: Rural consciousness and the power of perspective. *American Political Science Review, 106*(3), 517–532.

Cramer, K. J. (2016). *The politics of resentment: Rural consciousness in Wisconsin and the rise of Scott Walker.* University of Chicago Press.

Cremaschi, S., Rettl, P., Cappelluti, M., & De Vries, C. E. (2023). *Geographies of discontent: Public service deprivation and the rise of the far right in Italy.* Harvard Business School Working Paper 02-024.

Crulli, M. (2022). Vote metropolitanization after the transnational cleavage and the suburbanization of radical right populism: The cases of London and Rome. *Italian Journal of Electoral Studies, 85*(1), 3–23.

de Fine Licht, J., & Esaiasson, P. (2023). Att hantera svåra beslut–ett nödvändigt ont i den representativa demokratin. In B. P. Larsson (Ed.), *Hot mot det demokratiska samtalet – forskarantologi*. Sveriges Kommuner och Regioner.

de Fine Licht, J., Karlsson, D., & Skoog, L. (2023). Här, där eller överallt? Medborgares åsikter om lokalisering av offentlig service. In U. Andersson, P. Öhberg, A. Carlander, J. Martinsson, & N. Thorin (Eds.), *Ovisshetens tid*. The SOM-Institute, University of Gothenburg.

de Hoyos, M., & Green, A. (2011). Recruitment and retention issues in rural labour markets. *Journal of Rural Studies, 27*(2), 171–180.

Dijkstra, L., Poelman, H., & Rodríguez-Pose, A. (2020). The geography of EU discontent. *Regional Studies, 54*(6), 737–753.

Donatella, P., & Karlsson, D. (2023). Local politicians' perceptions of financial conditions – Do they align with financial indicators? *Local Government Studies.* Published online ahead of print.

Eidheim, M. R., & Fimreite, A. L. (2020). Geografisk konflikt i det politiske landskapet: En fortelling om to dimensjoner. *Norsk statsvitenskapelig tidsskrift, 36*(2), 56–78.

Fogelholm, P., de Fine Licht, J., & Esaiasson, P. (2019). *När beslutet fattats: en studie av kommuners hantering av skolnedläggningar*. School of Public Administration, University of Gothenburg.

Fredriksson, A. (2017). Location-allocation of public services – Citizen access, transparency and measurement. A method and evidence from Brazil and Sweden. *Socio-Economic Planning Sciences, 59*, 1–12.

Giancotti, M., Guglielmo, A., & Mauro, M. (2017). Efficiency and optimal size of hospitals: Results of a systematic search. *PloS One, 12*(3), e0174533.

Grzybowski, S., Stoll, K., & Kornelsen, J. (2011). Distance matters: A population based study examining access to maternity services for rural women. *BMC Health Services Research, 11*(1), 1–8.

Huijsmans, T. (2023). Place resentment in 'the places that don't matter': Explaining the geographic divide in populist and anti-immigration attitudes. *Acta Politica, 58*(2), 285–305.

Hutchcroft, P. D. (2001). Centralization and decentralization in administration and politics: Assessing territorial dimensions of authority and power. *Governance: An International Journal of Policy and Administration, 14*(1), 22–53.

Isaksson, Z. (2023). The political effects of rural school closures – Evidence from Sweden. *Journal of Rural Studies, 100,* 103009.

Jones, A., Rahman, R. J., & Jiaqing, O. (2019). A crisis in the countryside-Barriers to nurse recruitment and retention in rural areas of high-income countries: A qualitative meta-analysis. *Journal of Rural Studies, 72,* 153–163.

Karlsson, D. (2022). Lokalisering av offentlig service – ideologi och egenintresse. In P. Öhberg, H. Oscarsson, & J. Ahlbom (Eds.), *Folkviljans förverkligare.* University of Gothenburg.

Kearns, R. A., Lewis, N., McCreanor, T., & Witten, K. (2009). 'The status quo is not an option': Community impacts of school closure in South Taranaki, New Zealand. *Journal of Rural Studies, 25*(1), 131–140.

Kiewiet, D. R., & Lewis-Beck, M. S. (2011). No man is an island: Self-interest, the public interest and sociotropic voting. *Critical Review, 23*(3), 303–319.

Kinder, D. R., & Kiewiet, D. R. (1981). Sociotropic politics: The American case. *British Journal of Political Science, 11*(2), 129–161.

Kutsyuruba, B., Klinger, D. A., & Hussain, A. (2015). Relationships among school climate, school safety, and student achievement and well-being: A review of the literature. *Review of Education, 3*(2), 103–135.

Larsson Taghizadeh, J. (2016). *Power from below?: The impact of protests and lobbying on school closures in Sweden.* Doctoral dissertation, Uppsala University.

Lipset, S. M., & Rokkan, S. (1967). Cleavage structures, party systems and voter alignments: An introduction. In S. M. Lipset & S. Rokkan (Eds.), *Party systems and voter alignments* (pp. 1–64). Free Press.

Marshall, J. N. (2007). Public sector relocation policies in the UK and Ireland. *European Planning Studies, 15*(5), 645–666.

McCann, P. (2020). Perceptions of regional inequality and the geography of discontent: Insights from the UK. *Regional Studies, 54*(2), 256–267.

Meehl, P. E. (1977). The selfish voter paradox and the thrown-away vote argument. *American Political Science Review, 71*(1), 11–30.

Munis, B. K. (2022). Us over here versus them over there… literally: Measuring place resentment in American politics. *Political Behavior, 44*(3), 1057–1078.

Raggl, A. (2015). Teaching and learning in small rural primary schools in Austria and Switzerland—Opportunities and challenges from teachers' and students' perspectives. *International Journal of Educational Research, 74,* 127–135.

Rickardsson, J. (2021). The urban–rural divide in radical right populist support: The role of resident's characteristics, urbanization trends and public service supply. *The Annals of Regional Science, 67*(1), 211–242.

Rickardsson, J., Mellander, C., & Bjerke, L. (2021). The Stockholm syndrome: The view of the capital by the "Places Left Behind". *Cambridge Journal of Regions, Economy and Society, 14*(3), 601–617.

Rodríguez-Pose, A. (2018). The revenge of the places that don't matter (and what to do about it). *Cambridge Journal of Regions, Economy and Society, 11*(1), 189–209.

Rokkan, S. (1970). The growth and structuring of mass politics in Western Europe: Reflections of possible models of explanation. *Scandinavian Political Studies, 5*(A5), 65–83.

Saglie, J. (2023). Sentrum–periferi – en skillelinje i endring? In J. Bergh & A. Haugsgjerd (Eds.), *Politikk i urolige tider. En studie av stortingsvalget 2021* (pp. 276–304). Cappelen Damm Akademisk.

Saglie, J., Mörkenstam, U., & Bergh, J. (2020). Political cleavages in indigenous representation: The case of the Norwegian and Swedish Sámediggis. *Nationalism and Ethnic Politics, 26*(2), 105–125.

Skoog, L., & Karlsson, D. (2018). Causes of party conflicts in local politics. *Politics, 38*(2), 182–196.

Soja, E. W. (2013). *Seeking spatial justice* (Vol. 16). University of Minnesota Press.

Stein, J., Buck, M., & Bjørnå, H. (2021). The centre–periphery dimension and trust in politicians: The case of Norway. *Territory, Politics, Governance, 9*(1), 37–55.

Strandberg, K., & Berg, J. (2019). When reality strikes: Opinion changes among citizens and politicians during a deliberation on school closures. *International Political Science Review*, 1–17.

Stroppe, A. K. (2023). Left behind in a public services wasteland? On the accessibility of public services and political trust. *Political Geography, 105*, 102905.

Syed, S. T., Gerber, B. S., & Sharp, L. K. (2013). Traveling towards disease: Transportation barriers to health care access. *Journal of Community Health, 38*, 976–993.

Tieken, M. C., & Auldridge-Reveles, T. R. (2019). Rethinking the school closure research: School closure as spatial injustice. *Review of Educational Research, 89*(6), 917–953.

Uba, K. (2016). Protest against school closures in Sweden. In L. Bosi, M. Giugni, & K. Uba (Eds.), *The consequences of social movements: People, policies and institutions*. Cambridge University Press.

Vaughan, L., Edwards, N., Imison, C., & Collins, B. (2018). *Rethinking acute medical care in smaller hospitals*. Nuffield Trust.

Wallman Lundåsen, S. (2024). Rurality and discontent: Unraveling the context effects of living in rural districts in local elections on support for Sweden democrats. *Journal of Rural Studies, 106*, 103209.

Wallman Lundåsen, S., & Erlingsson, G. Ó. (2023). Perceived fairness of intra-municipal cohesion politics: Does place of residence affect party preferences? *Political Geography, 107*, 102994.

Whitehead, J., Pearson, A., Lawrenson, R., & Atatoa-Carr, P. (2019). How can the spatial equity of health services be defined and measured? A systematic review of spatial equity definitions and methods. *Journal of Health Services Research and Policy, 24*(4), 270–278.

CHAPTER 3

The Quest for Legitimacy

As we observed in the previous chapter, the policy area of location is fraught with clashing interests and value conflicts that pose significant challenges for a political system. Whatever decision is made in a location issue, the risk is that some groups will be deeply dissatisfied with the chosen solutions, and there is a subsequent risk that place-based resentment could fracture society. It is not straightforward for political actors to decide how to handle these issues or determine who should influence the decisions.

In light of these challenges, this chapter will explore the challenge of location decisions through the lens of legitimacy. We will discuss what we actually mean by legitimacy, why decision-makers should strive for legitimacy, how legitimacy can be generated and sustained, and which problems are associated with evaluating legitimacy.

WHAT IS LEGITIMACY?

One of the most central questions in theories of democracy is why anyone should follow orders or accept decisions that are against their preferences or even interests (e.g. Gibson et al., 2005). In other words, why should individuals consent to be governed, why do they comply with taxation, and why do they accept the specific organisational arrangements of public services?

Fear of violence or other kinds of punishment is, certainly, one answer. Historically, this was often the primary reason why people obeyed an authority. For instance, if an autocratic king decided that a defence installation or a customs station should be situated in a particular location, it was probably not within the realm of the people's imagination to even contemplate opposing this decision. In most modern democracies, governing solely based on power is, however, not a viable option. It would not only be inefficient, but it would also result in an insecure position for the ones in power. As Tyler (2006, p. 377) states, 'seeking to govern a society or manage an organisation based upon the possession of power alone first requires enormous expenditures of resources to create a credible system of surveillance through which to monitor public behaviour to punish rule violators.'

To be able to rule without resolving to pure force, it matters who makes a decision and how she does it. This brings us to legitimacy, which in its most general form can be described as 'a virtue of political institutions and of the decisions—about laws, policies, and candidates for political office—made within them' (Peter, 2017). This virtue manifests itself in a diffuse support (Easton, 1965), a reservoir of goodwill or support for institutions and authorities that makes it possible for authorities to, at least sometimes, make unpopular decisions without losing power or turning to use of brutal force. Instead, legitimacy makes people follow decisions and rules voluntarily—because they feel that they ought to—rather than out of fear (Tyler, 2006; Levi et al., 2009). Political theorists' debate whether democracy is needed for legitimacy or whether alternative decision-making procedures that produce equally good or even better outcomes can also be legitimate (e.g. Raz, 1995). In practice, however, democracy in some version is regarded a precondition of legitimacy by most contemporary scholars.

Legitimacy is often discussed in relation to trust and confidence. Although analytically distinct, these concepts tend to blend together in everyday speech. A reasonable distinction is that trusting someone means believing they will do something in a proper way, while legitimacy refers to their right to do it and whether the task is carried out in a rightful manner. The legitimacy of political decisions, therefore, derives from the decision-makers' right to act and the manner in which they carry out their duties. While some researchers treat trust primarily as a component or expression of legitimacy, others see legitimacy as a base for trust. For our purposes, it suffices to say that there tends to be a reciprocal relationship between the legitimacy of an authority and the trustworthiness of that authority, where trustworthiness is based on some kind of evaluation of the intentions, competences, and record of that authority (e.g. Levi et al., 2009; Norris, 2022). Thereby, we are not interested in trust in the form of blind faith in an authority but in trust in relation to authorities' claims to power and actions.

Normative and Empirical Legitimacy

At this point, an important distinction to be made is between normative and empirical—or descriptive—legitimacy (e.g. Peter, 2017). *Normative legitimacy* refers to what *is* legitimate based on some kind of predetermined criteria. Outcomes of democratic elections are an example. In liberal representative democracies, the general election is the stipulated mechanism by which a legitimate leader or government is determined. Once the election is completed (and any appeals are processed), the winner is proclaimed the legitimate authority. Competitors (with some notable exceptions) also tend to gracefully congratulate the legitimate winner. Similarly, in countries adhering to the norm of rule of law, a court's judgement determines what is right or wrong, who is guilty and who is not, within a certain jurisdiction. Notably, this also means that a de facto authority can be illegitimate. A ruler who gains power by illegal means, even if she is very competent, is not a legitimate leader. Similarly, a popular decision made by an unauthorised actor also lacks legitimacy. Legitimacy does not necessarily mean good.

But is ruling according to laws and regulations always the normative criterion for legitimacy? Not necessarily. Norms can clash. The purpose of normative theory is to determine what is right and what should be done, regardless of legal frameworks. By normative reasoning, it is possible to reach the conclusion that it is legitimate to break the law, for example to save lives or call attention to certain problems in society. Groups using civil disobedience as a method—such as those occupying a maternity ward to halt political closure decisions—often appeal to what they present as a higher-level criterion of legitimacy that trumps current legal bindings. Similarly, laws that are outdated and not in line with the moral standards of a modern society, for example laws that are discriminatory, can be changed as a result of developments in normative theory. Nevertheless, in practice, legality is often the prime criterion of legitimacy in democracies since until a law is removed, it is tied to the formal authority's monopoly of violence. Lawbreakers can be punished and detained by reference to the law, even if the purpose of their actions is benevolent.

Empirical—or descriptive—*legitimacy*, on the other hand, refers to what is *perceived* as legitimate by relevant actors. Usually, the concept includes both acceptance of authority and a felt obligation to obey that authority. In other words, to do as told because one feels that one should. This understanding of legitimacy can be traced back to Weber (1964) who defined legitimacy sociologically in terms of a *belief* in the rightness of an authority. This means that a leader can claim legitimacy based on other grounds than legality, such as charisma, religion, or tradition, as long as she can foster a belief in her legitimate authority.

At a glance, the distinction between normative and empirical legitimacy might seem overly technical. Logically, one may think that people's *perceptions* of what is legitimate should be based on what *is* legitimate. However, when it comes to the actual political reality and policy decisions being made, no such correlation is evident. In essence, people can *feel* that a decision is wrong—and act upon that feeling—even if it has been made by a formally legitimate decision-maker in a formally correct procedure. Similarly, people can accept decisions and policies they agree with, even if they are made in an inferior or even illegal way. The two types of legitimacy are also constantly conflated in both academic deliberations and more practice-based discussions on legitimate steering and governance.

Decisions on the location of public services bring this dilemma to fore. Take the example of a school closure in a small village, that is a typical case when a LALU is under threat. A local political board or council can be legally authorised to make decisions on the organisation of schools in the municipality and thus have a legitimate base for a decision to close the school. But for a parent who desperately wants her child to stay in the small, local, and well-known school under threat of closure, legality is not necessarily the concern. Instead, a moral component influences her assessment of the decision-makers. She may feel that public authorities simply do not have the right to close her child's school, because the decision is *wrong*. Her view might be that politicians do not understand the place they are making decisions about, that they do not care for the children in the village, or that they have not fully accounted for the consequences of such a decision for the community. By extension, such feelings can make her feel that she (and the group she belongs to) is not as valued as citizens. She may lose her confidence, not only in the current government but in the political system as such. This means that a democratically elected regime that makes a series of formally legitimate decisions, for example about the location of services, risks losing its (empirical) legitimacy if the people consider these decisions to be objectionable.

Many scholars argue that at least in the long run, it is not beneficial to regard legitimacy as something that is based either on legality *or* on beliefs (e.g. Beetham, 2013). Rather, legality or conformity to predetermined rules is a necessary condition, but to claim legitimacy, a regime also needs to grow a general belief in its legitimacy expressed in widespread public consent to its authority. In other words, an authority—even if it is appointed in a free and democratic election and installed according to all rules—cannot do whatever it wants and still claim legitimacy. It also needs to engender perceptions of acceptance or at least tolerance from its citizens while exercising its authority.

This brings us to the question of legitimacy in terms of substance and legitimacy in terms of procedures.

What Drives Legitimacy? A Question of Substance and Process

As we have touched upon already, we can distinguish between legitimacy based on *substance* and legitimacy based on *procedures*. Simply put, do we evaluate legitimacy by looking at final decisions or their results, for example whether a location decision that the authorities have made will provide the citizenry with satisfactory access to public services, or by assessing the process by which a decision came about, for example if the process followed legal requirements and allowed relevant stakeholders a say?

While the importance of substance is indisputable—after all, what matters most to our welfare is that we are provided with essential goods and services—the discussion on how to generate and sustain legitimacy, especially in issues relating to location decisions, often revolves around procedures in one way or another. A major reason is likely that from the politicians' and public officials' point of view, procedures are possible to do something about. As previously argued, under conditions of resource constraints, painful location decisions will be necessary. It will not be possible to only make popular decisions, for example to keep all service units that the people desire or provide no physical ground for a necessary yet unpopular facility. While still trying to make the wisest possible decision in terms of substance, decision-makers caring about public legitimacy may therefore turn their eyes to the process by which a location decision is made and hope that procedural perceptions will spill over to the judgement of the substance of the decision.

One way to think about democratic processes is elections, or what is sometimes referred to as the *input* side of politics. By participating in free and fair elections, the public chooses representatives who on their behalf make the decisions they deem needed during until called into account in the next election. This is the traditional idea of representative democracy (e.g. Manin, 1997; Urbinati & Warren, 2008).

In location decisions, the public input in the form of elections is, however, generally not the main issue. It certainly happens that a local election campaign is dominated by a specific policy issue like school reorganisation or infrastructure investment. But in most cases, specific location decisions arise within an electoral cycle where the election campaigns have focused on other, often more general, issues. When discussing procedures in relation to location decisions, it is therefore rarely enough to remind a potentially upset public that they had the opportunity to select their representatives in the latest general election and that these representatives have the formal mandate to decide. Rather, when discussing procedures in relation to specific policy decisions, like decisions on location of services, it is often the *throughput* side of politics, that is the quality of the decision-making processes once elections have been held (e.g. Schmidt & Wood, 2019), and the quality in the application of policies and laws (e.g. Rothstein, 2009), that comes into question. In other words, it matters not only who makes the decision but also *how* she does it.

Decision-making procedures are often evaluated in terms of their fairness. *Procedural fairness* (or justice) *theory* (e.g. Thibaut & Walker, 1975; Lind & Tyler, 1988; Tyler, 2006) has its roots in social psychology but has inspired political scientists and public administration scholars to study procedures and their effects on people's willingness to accept policies and trust decision-makers (e.g. Grimes, 2006; Esaiasson et al., 2019; Marien & Werner, 2019; Ruder & Woods, 2020; de Fine Licht et al., 2022). In its basic form, the theory states that people's willingness to accept decisions is influenced by their perceptions of the fairness of the procedures by which authorities make decisions. In primarily experimental studies mimicking situations where citizens interact with, for instance, a policeman, judge, or employer, it has been shown that people who feel that they have been fairly treated by, for example, being allowed to have a say in process, being treated with respect, and getting perceived sincere explanations, are more willing to also accept decisions that go against their preferences.

The procedural approach to legitimacy is obviously appealing. If the process is paramount for people's willingness to accept decisions, it is possible to gain legitimacy also for potentially controversial decisions like the location of wanted or unwanted facilities. It also speaks well to what Sabl (2005, p. 16) has named *democratic sportsmanship*, that is that democratic citizens must be good losers, willing to accept with good grace and no loss of commitment to the polity that the democratic game will not always go their way. Although not necessarily referring to procedural fairness theory as such, the underlying logic that process matters for legitimacy assessments have been highly influential in academic as well as policy-oriented discussions on how to build a sustainable democracy capable of meeting contemporary challenges. In particular, various forms of involving the public in decision-making (e.g. Dryzek et al., 2019; Werner & Marien, 2022) have been suggested as ways of enhancing decision-making quality and public trust in democratic institutions. We will return to these issues in Chap. 6.

Nevertheless, when applying a procedural approach to the political reality, at least two major problems arise. First, designing procedures for making collectively binding decisions is not necessarily as simple as applying successful ways of managing more personal relationships. For example, a central, if not the most central, operationalisation of fair procedures in the social psychological literature is *voice*, that is giving concerned actors an opportunity to have a say in the process (Van den Bos, 1999). However, it is a great challenge to give a whole population voice in a process such as, for example, a school closure. Not only does it require much more resources in terms of time and equipment to organise, for instance, a referendum or public meeting, but the prospects of actually reaching all individuals and make them aware of the efforts are low.

Second, even if agreement on principles can be reached, it is not evident how an actual procedure that will be accepted as fair should be designed. Some components in a correct process can certainly be codified in laws and regulations. This includes such things as who has the mandate to make decisions, who needs to be consulted, how documents underlying the decision should be made available, and how much time there must be between different stages in the process. Other components are, however, much more subtle. A general code of conduct for public officials can, for example, state that people trying to influence a location decision should be treated with respect, but what that means in an actual interaction between a politician and a citizen is difficult to specify.

Another complicating issue is that also the codified components of a process are open for interpretation, especially when translated into actual activities. Local politicians may, for example, think that they have fulfilled a regulated duty to consult with affected groups of citizens when they have organised a public meeting and listened to their arguments against a location decision. Still, in light of all considerations they may decide to go forward with an unpopular policy because they believe it is the right thing to do. While this is in line with representative responsiveness (e.g. Pitkin, 1967), the citizens attending such a meeting may feel that they were not listened to since the politicians obviously went ahead with a decision that is essentially *wrong*. In their view, the politicians had already made their decision, and the consultation was no more than a charade.

In essence, when people like policy outcomes and are on the 'winning' side of politics, they generally do not complain about potential flaws in a process. However, losers are generally hard to convince about the accuracy of the procedure. While most people in established democracies agree with the principle that one needs to accept decisions that go against one's preferences as long as the authority has followed standard procedures, losers facing a policy loss routinely tend to look for flaws in the decision-making procedure (Esaiasson et al., 2023). And as you search, you will find. There simply is no such thing as a perfect procedure—not for location decisions and not for any other controversial matter either. Details will be revealed that should never have been noticed or complained about if the process had resulted in what opposers—or losers—believe to be the right outcome.

Taken together, this means that a procedural approach to generating legitimacy for a location decision is far from as straightforward as it might seem.

A LULU Success? A Home for Young Male Refugees in a Wealthy Area

In a wealthy municipality near Stockholm, a house built for businesses in 1926 had been empty for several years. Its location by the busy road had always made it difficult to attract both office guests and restaurant owners. In a personal chronicle in one of the leading daily newspapers in Sweden (af Klintberg, 2023), a resident of the neighbourhood describes what happened during the refugee crisis of 2015 when the political leadership of the municipality came up with the proposal that the empty house should be turned into an asylum accommodation for unaccompanied refugee boys.

It soon became clear that the proposed home for young refugees was indeed considered what we would call a LULU by many residents in the area. One man in the neighbourhood quickly decided to collect a list of signatures protesting the proposal. A group of neighbours thereafter demanded a meeting with representatives from the municipality, raising issues from how the presence of the refugee home would affect the house prices in the neighbourhood (said by a lady in pearl necklace) to fear of safety for girls in the area (said by a father of daughters). The author of the chronicle, on the other hand, was one of few at the meeting who supported the establishment, to the price of angry looks from her neighbours.

This short story, which echoes many similar situations, shows how locating decisions can raise emotions such as fear and anger, cause heated protests, and split neighbourhoods. It also shows the power of NIMBY-ism. Many people at the meeting were probably in favour of helping refugees and would classify accommodations for refugees as necessary facilities *in principle* but still refused to have them near their own homes. One man at the hearing claimed, for instance, that he was against the accommodation mainly for the boys' own sake. According to him, the busy location by the road meant that it was directly unsuitable for children. This concern could, of course, be true, but it also reflects the creativity that tends to arise when there is a perceived need to keep a LULU away.

The story also speaks to the complexity of legitimacy. On the one hand, one might say that the proposal lacked legitimacy since it was not accepted by the population mostly affected by it. On the other

(continued)

(continued)
hand, if Sweden as a country, in line with national as well as internationals laws, has decided to welcome refugees, they need to have a place to stay. Why should wealthy neighbourhoods with strong resources to protest be excluded from that responsibility? And since those supporting the proposal (like the author of the chronicle) or do not care that much have less incentives to engage in the process, it is not certain that the highly critical group at the hearing were representative of the population in the neighbourhood.

Further, it is not clear when and how the legitimacy of the decision should be evaluated. In this case, the refugee home was actually established, despite the protests. The boys moved in, and the author of the chronicle describes how she and her husband went there to celebrate the pre-Christmas tradition of first advent. During the next years, she followed the boys' journey through the Swedish school system and society and saw how they managed to thrive despite their rough start. According to Statistics Sweden, that followed up on how things went for the unaccompanied children arriving in 2015 seven years later, the majority also turned out to receive high school degrees, and among those, 85 per cent had jobs. All in all, they were highly integrated. Does this mean that the decision to establish the home for the boys was right, despite initial criticism? From a normative perspective? From an efficiency perspective? Moreover, the story raises the question of who should be asked to evaluate the legitimacy of the decision. Previous residents of the neighbourhood? Current residents? Experts? These questions have no simple answer but are crucial for the long-term sustainability of the democratic system.

Evaluating Legitimacy

How can we determine if a decision, decision-maker, or process, for example in relation to a location decision, is legitimate? In many cases, it is comparatively easy to assess whether a decision or decision-making process is in line with laws and regulations. Protocols for determining aspects such as the transparency and integrity of the decision-making process can be established, and routines for securing the agreed-upon stages of the process can be implemented. At the extreme, a court can decide whether a decision is legal or not. But as previously argued, lawfulness is not everything. It is far more demanding to assess whether a decision is reasonable, appropriate, or, for that matter, fair. Many empirically oriented researchers and policymakers therefore resort to asking people what they think is legitimate. Notably, this is not necessarily because they think that legitimacy *is* the same as a belief in legitimacy, but because it is considered a reasonable way of measuring it.

What to ask people in order to find out whether they find a decision legitimate is, however, not a simple question. So far, there is no consensus on what a good measurement is. One concern is the role of fairness in relation to legitimacy. Even though it is often argued that legitimacy and fairness are distinct from each other (e.g. Levi et al., 2009; Peter, 2017), measures of legitimacy and trust often end up in referring to fairness in one way or another. The reason is likely that scholars are influenced by procedural fairness theory but also that it tends to reflect how ordinary citizens think and evaluate decisions and processes. Nevertheless, it questions the theoretical stringency of the empirical evaluations.

Another concern is whether legitimacy should be treated as a uniform evaluation or as one composed of different qualities. In experimental and survey-based research seeking to estimate perceptions of legitimacy, researchers often differentiate between evaluations of procedures, evolutions of particular decisions or outcomes, and evaluations of decision-makers and/or institutions (e.g. Herian et al., 2012; Esaiasson et al., 2019; Beyers & Arras, 2021; Marien & Werner, 2019; Ulbig, 2008; Ruder & Woods, 2020; Tyler, 1988). In theory, these concepts are indeed different qualities. It is possible, for example, to accept a decision resulting from a poor process, or not accept a decision based on a high-quality procedure. Moreover, in theory, these qualities come in a certain order. The logic of a procedural approach to legitimacy is that perceptions about the fairness of procedures will affect people's willingness to accept and trust decision-makers. That is, the evaluation of the process comes first, and it determines whether one will accept the outcome. A good procedure will make me accept any outcome, even if it is against my interests or preferences.

But in real-world policymaking, people are not always following the process of a decisions in detail. In some, or even many, cases the procedure does not even receive attention before an (unpopular) policy decision has been made. These cases may therefore result in reversed causality: the evaluation of the outcome—such as a decision to close a school—colours the evaluation of the process. The simple logic is that the 'bad' outcome must have been the result of a bad process. Alternatively, people do not make separate judgements of the process and the outcome, but simply form an opinion of the fairness of the whole. As, for example, Doherty and Wolak (2012) have shown, people are reasonably good at assessing the quality of a procedure when procedures are clearly fair or unfair. However, when the fairness of a process is ambiguous, which is often the case when location decisions are made, people are more likely to use their prior attitudes as a guide. This is by no means a problem specific to legitimacy measurement but rather to public opinion research in general, but it means that it is not always easy to say what is actually evaluated and, by extension, what the conclusions for policymaking strategies should be.

Further, a critical question is what it means to accept, respect, or tolerate a decision. Typically, researchers evaluate the outcome of a political procedure by asking people, for example, to what extent they agree with a location decision, accept the decision, or are prepared to follow the decision. More demanding forms of consent are also possible, like the extent to which one is prepared to protest—or defend—a decision. While justifiable as proxies for compliance in one form or another, these are, however, still *perceptions* and *intentions*, not actual behaviour. The question therefore arises if we should also look for evidence of actual compliance.

How evidence of actual compliance should look like is, however, not evident. Should, for instance, a heated protest against the establishment of a prison in an area be interpreted as a sign of an illegitimate process? Or alternatively, should a *lack* of heated protests necessarily be interpreted as a sign that the placement of the prison is perceived as legitimate? Scholars such as MacCoun (2005) have warned that the sword of procedural approaches to legitimacy is double-edged. A formally correct and 'fair' procedure can manipulate people into accepting rules and policies that are not in their interest. Especially in disadvantaged areas, the appearance of acceptance of a controversial location decision can hide inequalities in political resources, education, self-esteem, and available time for political work.

Related to the previous point, we have the question of *when* legitimacy should be evaluated. Evaluating legitimacy right after a potentially controversial policy decision bears the risk of exaggerating the magnitude of dissatisfaction. As, for example, Rothstein (2009) has argued, sometimes politicians make decisions that are not at all supported by that time, but where time shows that they were right. His example is the Swedish decision to introduce right-hand traffic, which was highly unpopular when the law was passed (after a referendum clearly said no), but then quickly changed into high public support once introduced. Similarly, Swedish experiences of structural reforms such as municipal amalgamations (or, for that matter, the EU membership) show that they are rarely popular when introduced, but acceptance grows over time. The same can be true for decisions on location. Take again the example of the closing of a small but popular village school. By the time of closing, children and their parents may experience stress from uncertainty and a general resistance to change, but these feelings may tune down as they get used to commuting and see the benefits of a larger and more centrally located school. At the same time, such growing of legitimacy over time cannot be taken for granted. It is also possible that experiences of heated and polarised conflicts can produce scars in a community that are hard to heal. If feelings of resentment and indignation grow, it can be devastating for democracy in the long run.

Finally, how do we determine the level of approval necessary to judge a process or decision as legitimate in the eyes of the public? It is uncontroversial to say that it is not possible to please all citizens, but is there a threshold for when disaffection becomes a problem? One answer could be electoral accountability. If a government elected by a majority of the people makes decisions that the public cannot bear with in the long run, they will be replaced. At the same time, just because one issue is not perceived as important enough by such a share of the population that it can swing the election result, it does not mean that it can be ignored. For a smaller yet substantial share of the population, a specific location issue can be very important. Not addressing such dissatisfaction can grow resentment and mistrust. At worst, it can result in continued protests delaying implementation or even threats against political representatives. Therefore, a simple majoritarian approach to legitimacy may not be sustainable.

While not an exhaustive list, these points show that evaluating legitimacy is a complex task, regardless of whether the purpose is academic or policy-oriented. But this does not mean that the work to enhance the prospects of gaining legitimacy for location decisions can be de-prioritised. In the years to come, decisions on the location of wanted as well as unwanted services are likely to be on top of the public debate, and the well-being of democracy depends on finding solutions that can secure public support.

SUMMARY

From this chapter, we learn that in one way or another, governments at all levels need to secure acceptance or at least tolerance for their decisions in the long run. Strictly following legal restrictions and formal protocols of decision-making is not enough, the outcomes of the processes also need to be legitimate in eyes of the public. This is not least the case for decisions on the location of public services as these are situations involve high stakes for affected citizens.

How to generate legitimacy is, however, not evident. Making only popular decisions is not an option. Legal requirements, budgetary constraints, and quality concerns will make painful decisions on location necessary. Neither is hoping that people will accept unwelcome decisions as long as they are made by a fair procedure a straightforward solution. For someone on the losing side in a sensitive issue, it is often very easy to find procedural flaws also in a highly transparent and inclusive process.

Decision-makers will have to navigate between different considerations to make the best possible (or the least bad) decision in the specific situation—for as many as possible and in the long run—but still need to prepare to meet disappointed citizens.

REFERENCES

af Klintberg, E. (2023, December 13). Fördomarna om pojkarna som kom kastas omkull. *Svenska Dagbladet*.

Beetham, D. (2013). *The legitimation of power*. Bloomsbury Publishing.

Beyers, J., & Arras, S. (2021). Stakeholder consultations and the legitimacy of regulatory decision-making: A survey experiment in Belgium. *Regulation and Governance*, 15(3), 877–893.

de Fine Licht, J., Agerberg, M., & Esaiasson, P. (2022). "It's not over when it's over"—Post-decision arrangements and empirical legitimacy. *Journal of Public Administration Research and Theory*, 32(1), 183–199.

Doherty, D., & Wolak, J. (2012). When do the ends justify the means? Evaluating procedural fairness. *Political Behavior*, 34(2), 301–323.

Dryzek, J. S., et al. (2019). The crisis of democracy and the science of deliberation. *Science*, 363(6432), 1144–1146.

Easton, D. (1965). *A systems analysis of political life*. Wiley.

Esaiasson, P., Persson, M., Gilljam, M., & Lindholm, T. (2019). Reconsidering the role of procedures for decision acceptance. *British Journal of Political Science*, 49(1), 291–314.

Esaiasson, P., Arnesen, S., & Werner, H. (2023). How to be gracious about political loss – The importance of good loser messages in policy controversies. *Comparative Political Studies, 56*(5), 599–624.

Gibson, J. L., Caldeira, G. A., & Spence, L. K. (2005). Why do people accept public policies they oppose? Testing legitimacy theory with a survey-based experiment. *Political Research Quarterly, 58*(2), 187–201.

Grimes, M. (2006). Organizing consent: The role of procedural fairness in political trust and compliance. *European Journal of Political Research, 45*(2), 285–315.

Herian, M. N., Hamm, J. A., Tomkins, A. J., & Pytlik Zillig, L. M. (2012). Public participation, procedural fairness, and evaluations of local governance: The moderating role of uncertainty. *Journal of Public Administration Research and Theory, 22*(4), 815–840.

Levi, M., Sacks, A., & Tyler, T. (2009). Conceptualizing legitimacy, measuring legitimating beliefs. *American Behavioral Scientist, 53*(3), 354–375.

Lind, E. A., & Tyler, T. R. (1988). *The social psychology of procedural justice.* Plenum Press.

MacCoun, R. J. (2005). Voice, control, and belonging: The double-edged sword of procedural fairness. *Annual Review of Law and Social Science, 1*, 171–201.

Manin, B. (1997). *The principles of representative government.* Cambridge University Press.

Marien, S., & Werner, H. (2019). Fair treatment, fair play? The relationship between fair treatment perceptions, political trust and compliant and cooperative attitudes cross-nationally. *European Journal of Political Research, 58*(1), 72–95.

Norris, P. (2022). *In praise of skepticism: Trust but verify.* Oxford University Press.

Peter, F. (2017). Political legitimacy. In E. N. Zalta (Ed.), *The Stanford encyclopedia of philosophy* (Summer 2017 ed.) Retrieved March 13, 2024, from https://plato.stanford.edu/archives/sum2017/entries/legitimacy/

Pitkin, H. (1967). *The concept of representation.* University of California Press.

Raz, J. (1995). *Ethics in the public domain: Essays in the morality of law and politics.* Clarendon Press.

Rothstein, B. (2009). Creating political legitimacy: Electoral democracy versus quality of government. *American Behavioral Scientist, 53*(3), 311–330.

Ruder, A. I., & Woods, N. D. (2020). Procedural fairness and the legitimacy of agency rulemaking. *Journal of Public Administration Research and Theory, 30*(3), 400–414.

Sabl, A. (2005). Virtue for pluralists. *Journal of Moral Philosophy, 2*(2), 207–235.

Schmidt, V., & Wood, M. (2019). Conceptualizing throughput legitimacy: Procedural mechanisms of accountability, transparency, inclusiveness and openness in EU governance. *Public Administration, 97*(4), 727–740.

Thibaut, J. W., & Walker, L. (1975). *Procedural justice: A psychological analysis.* Erlbaum.

Tyler, T. R. (1988). What is procedural justice-criteria used by citizens to assess the fairness of legal procedures. *Law & Society Review, 22*, 103.

Tyler, T. R. (2006). Psychological perspectives on legitimacy and legitimation. *Annual Review of Psychology, 57*, 375–400.

Ulbig, S. G. (2008). Voice is not enough: The importance of influence in political trust and policy assessments. *Public Opinion Quarterly, 72*(3), 523–539.

Urbinati, N., & Warren, M. E. (2008). The concept of representation in contemporary democratic theory. *Annual Review of Political Science, 11*, 387–412.

Van den Bos, K. (1999). What are we talking about when we talk about no-voice procedures? On the psychology of the fair outcome effect. *Journal of Experimental Social Psychology, 35*(6), 560–577.

Weber, M. (1964). *The theory of social and economic organization*. Free Press.

Werner, H., & Marien, S. (2022). Process vs. outcome? How to evaluate the effects of participatory processes on legitimacy perceptions. *British Journal of Political Science, 52*(1), 429–436.

CHAPTER 4

Location in a Multilevel Setting

Political leaders and heads of public agencies are responsible for making decisions on location of public services and facilities. They must navigate the interest and value conflicts associated with the centre-periphery divide as outlined in Chap. 2 and as well as demands for legitimacy as presented in Chap. 3. In this chapter, we discuss how the construction of the political system influences how issues are handled and discuss the challenge of locating public services and facilities from an institutional and structural perspective.

When designing political systems, a core issue concerns the distribution of power and influence among actors and institutions on different tiers of government, captured by the concept of multilevel government. This is closely linked to the extent to which the multilevel system should promote either a strong local self-governance for sub-national units or rather promote national equity. The way multilevel systems are structured not only has implications for the management and organisation of various types of public services but has particular consequences for decisions regarding their geographical location. The size of the territorial units within the multilevel system plays a crucial role, and historical institutional reforms significantly shape the political leeway in location issues. Making the balance between what is considered a public and private responsibility a critical consideration.

Local Self-Governance Versus National Equity

Democracy foundation is the principle that those residing within a territory should have the power to influence its governance. In democratic theory, the term 'demos', borrowed from Ancient Greek, represents the body of people governing themselves in a democratic manner. Defining the demos is a timeless question within democratic studies. Embedded in this inquiry is one of democracy's oldest and most challenging dilemmas: which individuals constitute the self-governing people (Maltais et al., 2019)?

According to one perspective, offered by the American political scientist Robert Dahl (1989), all adults affected by a particular political decision should be included within the demos responsible for that decision. Importantly, this view implicitly suggests that individuals not affected by such a decision should not be part of the decision-making demos. The crux is that different political decisions impact various segments of the population to different extents. So, while this principle may appear simple, its practical implementation is seldom straightforward.

A potential solution to this democratic challenge is the adoption of a multilevel government system, where each tier of government is given a certain degree of political responsibility and autonomy. This means that allocation of political responsibility and self-governance to local and regional tiers of government is a way to solve the age-old question of how to closely match the decision-making demos with the population impacted by those decisions. It is hoped that politics, when carried out at a local level and in close proximity to its citizens, can be more democratic and responsive to local conditions and political sentiments (Erlingsson & Ödalen, 2017).

However, an anticipated (though not automatic) consequence of having a decentralised political system is: service variation. This means that self-governance undoubtedly opens for public services and infrastructures to be produced and managed differently, in various forms, with differing priorities, and varying levels of ambition across municipalities and regions. The challenge is that this service variation could potentially conflict with another highly regarded political value: national equity—the principle that all citizens should be treated equally and receive equitable services from the public sector (Karlsson, 2015).

This means that decentralised decision-making challenges the principle of uniform service provision for all citizens, potentially spurring debates, and perceptions of unequal treatment or even discrimination among citizens based on their place of residence. Consequently, the decentralisation of power through local autonomy, the pursuit of national equitability, and the decentralisation of services to promote accessibility are interrelated and must be balanced. Within the Nordic context, these tensions are heightened by two aspects: first, responsibilities for public services in Nordic countries are extensively decentralised to regional and local levels; second, Nordic welfare states are by tradition heavily anchored in egalitarian ideals (Esping-Andersen, 1990).

Questions regarding location of public services sit at the heart of the tension between self-governance and equity. Spatial allocation of such facilities is a key indicator against which equity is measured, as disparities in access to the nearest service unit often are perceived as problematic. Furthermore, the level at which decisions about location are made—locally or nationally—likely has significant consequences for how values are balanced against economic efficiency. Individuals who prioritise equity and are critical of service variation due to disparate municipal decisions may view centralised decision-making as a path towards greater equality. Thus, in a system that highlights decentralised service provision and social equality, political leaders across all tiers of government and politics face a delicate balancing act. To answer this, we have the opportunity to analyse results from surveys targeted at Swedish politicians on this issue.

During the first part of the twenty-first century, surveys have repeatedly asked Swedish elected representatives at local, regional, and national levels to weigh in on the balance between local self-governance and equitable services (Karlsson, 2022a). The results are summarised in Fig. 4.1.

The results depicted in Fig. 4.1 indicate a strong support among regional and local politicians in Sweden for promoting local autonomy. Conversely, national MPs in the *Riksdag* display ambivalence: approximately equal numbers are in favour of promoting local self-governance as are critical of it, and this stance has remained consistent over time. It is perhaps unsurprising that local and regional politicians desire reduced state influence over their affairs. However, of greater significance are the findings in Fig. 4.1 that demonstrate a decline in support for local autonomy among both local and regional politicians during the 2010s. This shift towards a more sceptical perspective on local self-governance has also been observed in other studies amongst local bureaucrats in Sweden (Johansson et al., 2018).

Another striking observation is a marked shift towards advocating equitable service provision nationwide. In 2008, the support for promoting

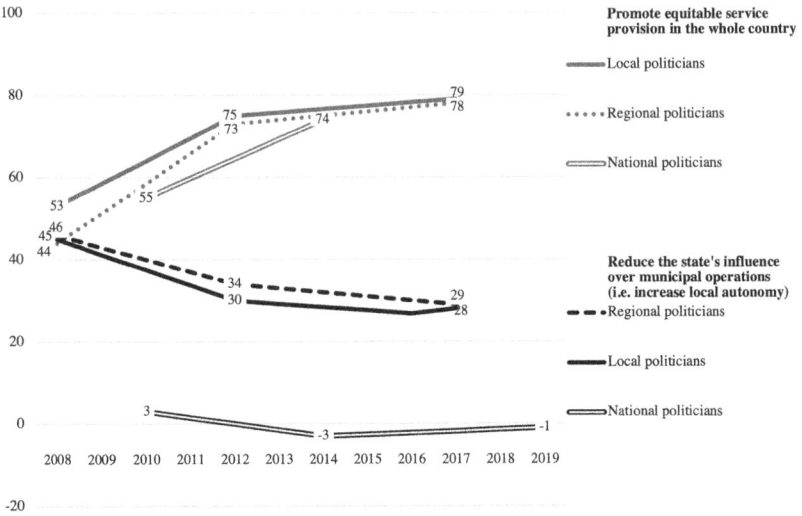

Fig. 4.1 Changes in Swedish politicians' views on self-governance and equality 2008–2019 (balance: positive-negative). (Sources: For national politicians: RDU 2010, 2014, 2019 (see Karlsson, 2018; Öhberg et al., 2022); for local and regional politicians: KOLFU 2008, 2012, 2017 (see Gilljam et al., 2010; Karlsson & Gilljam, 2014; Karlsson, 2017). Adapted from Karlsson (2022a). *Note*: The figure presents a balance measure, specifically the proportion of politicians who believe the cited proposals are very bad or fairly bad subtracted from the proportion who consider it fairly good or very good)

local autonomy and heightened equity were approximately on par, but the change in the following years has been great and is visible across all political parties and tiers of government. Today, promoting equitable service provision is a dominant position in Swedish politics. However, the interpretation of 'equitability' varies considerably. Debates on the topic involve a broad range of aspects such as identical financial provisions, service quality, or outcomes. Different political parties, naturally, provide different answers.

The dilemma is that support for local self-governance, that inevitably leads to service variation, is inherently in conflict with the ideal of equitable service provision. Thus, politicians are presented with a choice: either embrace—or at least tolerate—local variations in service standards based on adaption to local conditions or enforce national control and centralise services. Recent political debates indicate a preference among national actors in Sweden for the latter, with some experts cautioning against this approach's potential to undermine local autonomy.

However, the relationship between support for local autonomy and equitable service provision might be even more intricate. Though they are often seen as opposing goals, survey results show that a majority of politicians support both. Most municipal and regional politicians advocating for stronger local autonomy also support service equitability. A possible interpretation of this seemingly paradoxical stance is that equity is interpreted less as uniformity and more as achieving the best possible service quality given the unique conditions of each municipality and region. From this perspective, self-governance emerges as a possible tool to attain such optimality. Furthermore, centralised control by no means ensures uniformity. There are ample examples of regional service discrepancies in Sweden, even within services overseen by national authorities. Rather than nationalising responsibilities, a more effective strategy for achieving nationwide service equity might be to tackle the structural conditions that result in undesirable variations among municipalities (Lidström, 2022).

Multilevel Governance

Distribution of authority and influence between tiers of government stand at the core of multilevel government. But it is about much more than formal hierarchical relationships. Much of the decision-making that actually takes place in a multilevel system is informal, non-hierarchical, and highly dependent on network contacts. The term created to capture this phenomenon is 'multilevel governance' (rather than govern*ment*), which emerged within research on EU policy (Marks, 1993; Hooghe & Marks, 2003). This discussion delves into the significance of multilevel governance in the context of decisions regarding the location of public services and infrastructure.

Historical applications of multilevel governance (MLG) emphasise collaboration between EU and state-level institutions; the concept has since expanded to include the intricate relationships across tiers of government—international, national, regional, local—as well as private entities, as well as civil actors. A notable aspect of MLG is its relevance to the location of public services and facilities. Decisions related to these aspects occur at different tiers of government. Studies such as Karlsson (2022b), Marshall et al. (2005; Marshall, 2007), Nilsson and Lundgren (2015), and de Fine Licht et al. (2023) have explored the role of different tiers of government for the spatial distribution or allocation of public services.

Despite the tendency within bureaucratic systems to view local institutions as mere service providers implementing decisions made at national level, all political issues have reach downwards, upwards, and outwards. While decisions such as location of LALUs or LULUs that might be made at local level, they are not merely a technical matter, and these decisions has reached beyond a specific locality. Sellers et al. (2020) argue that decisions made by municipalities on issues such as location of services can be as influential as national politics in shaping the overall direction of the state and that we hence must 'take local institutions seriously'. This perspective challenges the predominant top-down view of politics often reinforced by research focusing on national politics. But each tier of government operates within territorial units that are unique in their composition of corporations, organisations, social groups, and citizens. And the decision-making processes at each of these levels are characterised by contestation and power dynamics. Thus, the importance of understanding the local dimension of governance is due to the unique mix of actors at the local level that contribute to the shaping of policies and services.

Multilevel governance is not uniformly apparent across all policy sectors, but its influence is pervasive. Policy sectors such as developmental policies (c.f. Svensson, 2019; Syssner, 2020; Wänström & Persson, 2023), environmental policies (c.f. Hansson-Forman et al., 2021), crisis management policies (c.f. Strandh, 2023), transportation and road policies (c.f. Hysing, 2022), and migration policies (Lidén & Nyhlén, 2023; Spehar et al., 2017) are often cited as prime examples of multilevel governance due to the territorial dilemmas inherent in these areas. However, multilevel arrangements can be found across all policy sectors, with each sector and government tier having services or infrastructure that require a physical facility or presence. Table 4.1 exemplifies how services within three sectors are distributed between national, regional, and local tiers of government in the case of Sweden. This illustrates that MLG is of importance even for policy sectors not commonly cited as prime examples of MLG.

The question of where activities should physically take place is a crucial consideration that becomes particularly pronounced when it comes to delivering services and infrastructure, as the physical location plays a pivotal role in shaping the effectiveness of these services. The debate revolves around the tension between two fundamental approaches: centralisation for efficiency (creating economies of scale) and decentralisation for local adaptation, while centralising responsibility for a policy area to a higher tier of government does not automatically lead to a concentration in the spatial

Table 4.1 Distribution of responsibilities in three public service sectors between tiers of government in Sweden

	Educational sector	*Healthcare sector*	*Public transport sector*
National level	Universities, Board of Student Finances, Swedish Higher Education Authority, Council for Higher Education	Research, Medical Guidelines and Educations, The National Board of Social Affairs and Health, The Health and Social Care Inspectorate	Trains, railways, airports
Regional (county) level	Colleges for adult education, lower healthcare education institutions	Hospitals, primary care centres, psychiatric care	Commuter services, bus lines, and commuter trains
Local (municipal) level	Secondary schools, primary schools, nurseries	Elderly care, social care services, disability support	Mobility services, school transportation services

allocation of services. In Sweden, for instance, where regions are responsible for healthcare, it can still mean that primary care centres operated by regional authorities are evenly distributed in the area. However, experience tells us that when services are centralised to a higher level of the multilevel system, a concentration of services in the centre is often a likely outcome.

Public, Private, or Civil Sector Responsibility for Service Provision

In Chap. 1 (Fig. 1.2), we introduced an analytical perspective on location issues, which partly related to whether the service or facility to be located is attractive to the local population or not (LALU/LULU) and partly to whether the facility is more or less necessary. One way to interpret the latter aspect is that for a municipality, certain facilities such as schools are necessary as all children need education but also because the law (at least in the Swedish case) demands that all municipalities provide schools. Another way to interpret the dimension is whether it is necessary for *the public sector* to provide the service. According to the prevailing social contract, some service activities have come to be defined as a public obligation, while others are expected to be managed by the private market.

Over the past four decades, the demarcation between public and private responsibilities has been increasingly blurred. Numerous countries have undergone a shift where their public sectors have been influenced by a market-driven approach through the implementation of reforms falling under the framework of New Public Management (NPM) (Hood, 1991; Pollitt & Bouckaert, 2017). Even though claims have been made that NPM is dead (Dunleavy et al., 2006), there is plenty of evidence for arguing that NPM is very much alive (Funck & Karlsson, 2020). This means that the traditional, hierarchical, rule-bound 'Weberian'—or 'old'—public administrations where focus was on processes, to varying extents, have given way to a results-focused public management. This shift has included a development where for-profit private enterprises and/or non-governmental organisations (NGOs) since the late 1970s to a greater extent have become responsible for matters that previously were viewed a responsibility for the public sector alone—such as provision of schools or hospitals. Effects and consequences of NPM vary between countries, and political actors respond differently to them (e.g. Skoog & Svärd, 2023), but this is most likely due to the variation between contexts where NPM-inspired reforms have been implemented (Lapuente & Van de Walle, 2020).

While outsourcing of public services is at times conditioned to take place in existing facilities, meaning that the public sector may have the ability to influence their location, but often non-public service providers have greater freedom to determine the locations for establishing their operations. And in theory, one might suppose that if small rural municipalities struggle to employ qualified personnel, they will benefit more from procuring private services. But the preconditions and ability to introduce competition and market-based solutions such as outsourcing operations to private contractors vary dramatically between urban and rural areas. There are also indications that non-public providers tend to prefer to be established in larger cities or urban areas (Jansson et al., 2021; Tillväxtverket., 2021).

Researchers argue that this establishment pattern jeopardises a political ideal of equity in service provision in the periphery. For instance, a Swedish study on healthcare provision in rural areas highlights an inherent contradiction between a political goal of equal access to health services and implementation of market-orienting reforms. As private healthcare providers have an economic incentive to locate their operations, where there are more patients and demands less resources to operate, they primarily choose to establish in densely populated cities and urban areas—leaving rural areas with lower access to healthcare (Kullberg et al., 2018). One reason for this establishment pattern is that smaller populations in rural areas risk hampering profit, making it simply not as financially attractive to operate in these places. This pattern can also be seen in urban areas where, for example, private schools prefer attractive locations in the city centre, leaving public schools to take care of education in resource-poor suburbs (Larsson & Hultqvist, 2018).

Moreover, in regions characterised by sparse populations and perhaps even population decline, the challenge of recruiting and retaining proficient personnel impedes provision of public services. Constrained economic resources due to diminished tax base means restricted fiscal capacities for developing—or even sustaining—service quality. This means that there are situations, where both public and for-profit private actors struggle to provide service of reasonable quality. Such situations may call for heightened involvement of non-profit or civil society organisations. Collaborations between public, private as well as civil sectors are common—indeed, to secure provision of services and infrastructure in peripheral regions they may even be a necessity. Civil society, such as parent associations, village communities, road associations, at times mobilise to form local associations with the goal of providing services and infrastructure, both replacing traditionally public and private tasks. For example, there are attempts for civil society to provide primary care (e.g. Cras, 2017; Forsberg, 2010; Lindberg, 2005) and broadband (Salemink et al., 2017).

Occasionally, the conventional understanding of what constitutes a public responsibility undergoes a re-evaluation. Consider, for example, grocery stores—quintessential private enterprises primarily engaged in selling food and household items. However, in sparsely populated regions, these stores occasionally extend their services beyond typical commercial activities, venturing into domains more traditionally associated with the public sector. This can include acting as agents for postal services, providing pharmacy services, and often serving as hubs for municipal information. In Sweden, they frequently also function as service points for the state-owned alcohol retail monopoly: Systembolaget. Moreover, these grocery stores play a significant social role as they often have designated spaces for café operations and, in some instances, even host meeting venues for local associations (Cras et al., 2023; Tillväxtverket., 2021). Those operating these establishments also often find themselves assuming additional roles, both self-imposed and occasionally those forced on them, where they are called upon to assist with tasks such as repairing broken-down cars, serving as tourist information points, and aiding elderly citizens with digital challenges (Strandh, 2023). This means that private businesses at times provide a great deal of public services. Indeed, the scenario can sometimes be inverted—when the final private grocery store ceases operations in a rural village, the municipality often finds itself under pressure to devise new solutions. In particularly acute situations, they may even step in to offer food retail services to local communities. Additionally, there are tax-financed subsidies in place to support stores that serve as the only commercial lifelines in rural areas devoid of other alternatives (Hammarlund & Nordin, 2023).

> **Location of LULU in a Multilevel Setting: The Case of Wind Turbines**
> An illustrative example of how location of public services and infrastructures is affected by the institutional arrangements of a multilevel system is the placement of wind energy turbines (Niskanen et al., 2024), often spurring tensions between urban and rural areas (Walker et al., 2018) and so-called not in my backyard-sentiments (Wolsink, 2000). In the Swedish context, the topic of wind farms is increasingly contested. While wind energy is broadly supported in Swedish public opinion as a clean, non-fossil energy source that does not contribute to climate change, protagonists of wind farms also often argue that the vast, sparsely populated Swedish landscape with its extensive coastlines is ideally suited for wind energy development. Critics, on the other hand, argue that the national climate objectives are overambitious. Here, wind farms often symbolise such overreach by the government, with the core of the critique focusing on their placement. Wind turbines are a quintessential LULU facility that are accused of marring picturesque landscapes, producing noise pollution, disrupting wildlife, and posing risks to aviation (Lindvall, 2023).
>
> Energy production is recognised as a public good, a prerequisite for a thriving modern society, at both national and even international levels. Yet, while energy production benefits the collective, it does not necessarily provide specific advantages to those residing near power plants. In contrast to other kinds of energy production, wind turbines are not associated with local economic benefits or local job opportunities that might mitigate negative feelings from citizens (Bidwell, 2013). However, Sweden largely relies on hydroelectric plants in the north and nuclear facilities in the south for its energy.
>
> *(continued)*

(continued)

Transmitting electricity to areas without such facilities is costly and logistically challenging, often hampered by so-called bottlenecks. In harsh winters, regions lacking energy production nearby may experience power shortages. Thus, having wind farms nearby can be seen as beneficial for a region.

Wind farm locations are increasingly contentious in Swedish local politics. Some municipalities are constructing their own turbines, others are welcoming private wind farms, others are resisting the establishment of such installations within their boundaries. Formally, urban planning and the issuing of construction permits in Sweden are under local authority. There is also a controversial 'municipal veto' at play, which allows municipalities to block the establishment of wind turbines by private energy companies within their territories. The inclination of many municipalities to decline wind turbine projects is viewed by proponents as an impediment to national energy strategies and Sweden's commitment to fulfilling international climate targets.

Sofia Axelsson et al. (2023) have delved into public sentiment on the siting of wind turbines and, importantly, have investigated which stakeholders the public believes should wield more or less influence over such decisions. Their findings paint a complex picture where citizens feel that both central and local actors should have a say in the placement of wind farms. Notably, there is a pronounced preference for local entities and groups such as municipalities, local residents, and especially private landowners to have significant influence, over and above national authorities (see Fig. 4.2).

There are also some intriguing distinctions between supporters and opponents of wind energy (Axelsson, 2023). Supporters lean towards central and industry influence, while opponents lean towards influence from local citizens and private landowners, likely because they believe such distribution of influence would produce policies aligned with their perspectives. Additionally, there is strong support for compensating municipalities and individuals residing near wind turbines. Such proposals have been discussed in the national political debate (Lindvall, 2023), and the popularity of these policies suggests that a buy-out strategy could potentially ease the location of LULU facilities more broadly.

(continued)

(continued)

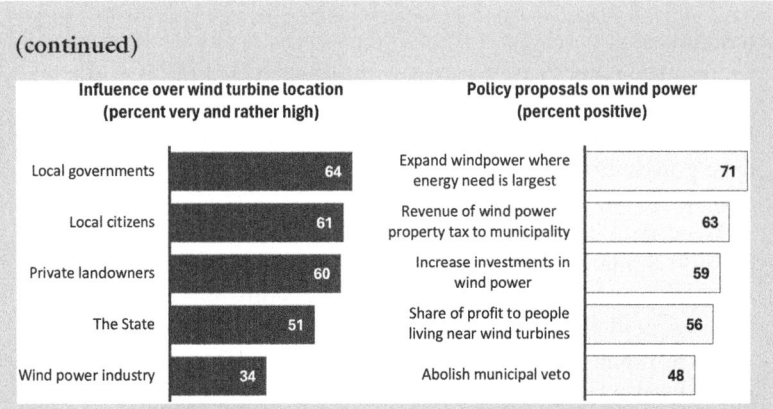

Fig. 4.2 Swedish public opinion on wind power issues. (*Note*: Results from the National SOM survey 2022 (Axelsson et al., 2023). In the Swedish Context, 'the state' refers to the government and authorities at the national level)

The case of wind turbines in Sweden demonstrates how the structure of the multilevel system influences siting decisions, and how citizens appear to favour institutional solutions and the allocation of political power and responsibility across different levels of government. These preferences are based on their perceptions of how such institutional frameworks would impact location decisions, both on a broad scale and within their own local areas.

The Size of a Polity

A central aspect for location decisions is the size of the polity that makes the decisions. If the decisions are made in a larger polity, for example at the regional or national level instead of in a municipality, the choices in terms of spatial allocation are much broader—whereas in a smaller polity, the decisions might rather concern maintaining or closing down a service unit. On the other hand, the insights into the decision's significance for the local community are greater when it is made in a smaller polity, close to those the issue concerns.

One crucial aspect of a polity's size concerns its significance for democratic processes and thus for shaping the procedures that lend legitimacy to location decisions. There are extensive debates on the benefits of both small and large entities, focusing on their capacity to deliver efficient, high-quality services as well as sustain a well-functioning democratic government. Dahl and Tufte (1973) introduced two critical perspectives to examine this dynamic: the system capacity and democracy perspectives, offering a framework to analyse the relationship between polity size and its impact on governance and service provision. When polities are too small, they may lack system capacity, that is the capability to enact political decisions. On the other hand, small scale can benefit grassroots participation in decision-making processes, which proponents argue may enhance the quality of democracy. However, such positive effects on democracy of smallness are by no means a given (Karlsson, 2013).

In local government studies, the size of municipalities is often a key factor in explaining policy and service delivery variations. Denters et al. (2014) suggest considering the effects of size as a 'funnel of causality', where political behaviour is influenced by various factors such as background, social orientation, and political preferences. They propose that size acts as a driving force, influencing these factors and thereby indirectly creating differences in democratic governance and political behaviour among individuals based on whether they reside in small or large polities. But size is not a static state—polities can increase or decrease their population over time, and the demographic composition of people may change. And such changes are among the most consequential factors when it comes to determining the need for public services and location politics. In many Western countries, rural and already sparsely populated areas are experiencing both an ageing population and a decline in numbers, while populous urban areas are growing even larger (Syssner, 2020). Essential services such as healthcare, education, and infrastructure may face challenges in maintaining a robust presence in depopulated areas. Moreover, the diminishing local tax base resulting from depopulation may lead to potential cutbacks in local welfare services.

When demographic changes are accentuating disparities between communities (Erlingsson et al., 2021), the urgency of rethinking location strategies increases. And where service facilities should be located becomes not just a question of adapting operations to the changes but also a way to counteract the development, maintaining services in a shrinking location can be a strategy to counteract out-migration. An even more drastic strategy to tackle the problems is to review the entire structural construction of the multilevel system, both in terms of the size of the units and their responsibilities.

Structural Reforms, Amalgamations, and Tensions Within Municipalities

When conditions for effective governance and a well-functioning democracy change—or when views on how best to achieve this evolve—a demand for reforms often arise. In recent years many structural reforms have been implemented around the world, where municipalities and regions have been altered. Normally—but not always—these are amalgamation reforms where polities are merged into larger units that meet the requirements for viable system capacity (Galizzi et al., 2023; Swianiewicz, 2018; Swianiewicz et al., 2017; Baldersheim & Rose, 2010). Questions about spatial allocation of public services are high on the agenda when such reforms are discussed, and these reforms give rise to the question of where service units should be placed.

A crucial question for location strategies during the implementation of structural reforms concerns whether political units at the same tier of government ought to have identical status and responsibilities, or alternatively, whether larger units should be expected to shoulder more responsibility than smaller ones. The terms 'symmetry' and 'asymmetry' are used to characterise these two distinct approaches to distributing power and authority among units within the same government tier. Where symmetry is found in unitary systems of most European countries, asymmetric division of power and authority have been applied more frequently in system where there has been a political desire to grant ethnic minorities varying degrees of, local or regional, self-rule. In the European countries, this is most pronounced in federal systems such as Switzerland, Belgium, and Bosnia-Hercegovina. But there are also unitary states where regions have been given far reaching self-rule, sometimes termed 'devolution', for example Åland in Finland, Scotland in the UK, Catalonia, and the Basque Country in Spain, etc. Thus, what tier is entrusted with responsibility for the provision of different public services such as schools, hospitals, and police may vary both within and between countries (Lidström, 2018).

Today, Sweden has a symmetric local government system where all municipalities and regions have the same responsibility for provision of welfare services regardless of variations in geography and demography. However, before a structural reform in the 1970s, the system was decidedly asymmetric at the local level. Meaning that depending on their relative sizes, municipalities had varying degrees of authority and responsibility. An inspiration for the unitary structure of the 'new' municipalities in Sweden was Walter Christaller's (1966) *Central Place Theory*. This spatial economic theory explains the distribution of human settlements and the arrangement of economic activities in a hierarchical order. Central place theory is particularly focused on the location and size of central places (urban centres or settlements) within a polity. These central places should be the dominant administrative place and provide goods and services to the surrounding population. In addition, the theory argues that for each service, there should be market or catchment areas reflecting the maximum distance people are willing to travel. As the structure of the 'new' Swedish municipalities was inspired by this theory, this meant that every new municipality was assigned a 'central place' (Swedish: *centralort*), that is a dominating town or city. Thus, as the number of municipalities decreased radically, a vast number of dominating towns saw their status and power drop, and many inhabitants of what recently were prominent local centres now found themselves living in new peripheries—with loss of status and an increased distances to public services (Erlingsson et al., 2023). The Swedish structural reform in the 1970s is therefore a prime example of how provision of public services brings tensions between centre and periphery to fore, with repercussions that are still palpable today.

Prime arguments for implementing amalgamation reforms are to increase efficiency and save costs (Leach & Copus, 2023). But the empirical evidence for such expectations is very much debated. While there may be some cost reductions for expenditures on general administration, these savings are frequently offset by higher expenditures on other public services. In addition, even though larger municipalities are argued to provide better services, satisfaction with services may decrease after amalgamations (Galizzi et al., 2023). Here, insights from the Icelandic amalgamation experiences of the 1990s might provide important nuances. While a general improvement in the quality of public services was perceived by the Icelanders, this enhancement was notably concentrated among those residing near municipal centres. Simultaneously, an uptick in tensions between the central hubs and peripheral regions of the new municipalities was observed. Residents and political representatives in peripheries expressed dissatisfaction with the development of public services within the larger, amalgamated municipality (Eythórsson & Karlsson, 2018). The potential for amalgamations to give rise to geographical tensions in the new and enlarged municipality is recognised by several scholars. This may arise when towns or cities after amalgamation reforms are, to a varying extent, formally designated as political and administrative centres within the newly expanded units, simultaneously demoting others to the status of peripheries (Erlingsson et al., 2023; Gendźwiłł et al., 2021). In addition, geographical tensions may be spurred by the risk that amalgamations could hamper the link between citizens' local identity and their attachment to their municipality (Hansen & Kjaer, 2020; Leach & Copus, 2023).

A study on the Finnish municipal amalgamation reform illustrates the complexities surrounding implementation of these reforms for public professionals. Harjunen et al. (2021) found that these reforms may lead to significant decreases in local public sector employment—particular within administration, social services, and healthcare. This means that public employees might find themselves compelled to relocate to areas with greater employment opportunities such as municipal or regional centres. This underlines the dual role of public officials, where they are both public employees and citizens. The potential for heightened job insecurity, due to amalgamation reforms or closure of a service unit where they are employed, may cause ambiguous attitudes amongst public employees, ranging from cautious support for reform to overt resistance.

Summary

In this chapter, we have observed how institutional and structural conditions influence the politics of service location. The design of a multilevel government system creates a structure of opportunities that delineates what is necessary, desirable, and possible. Notably, the degree of self-governance and the perspective on equity play a crucial role. However, as the case of wind power illustrates, the relationship between institutions and location decisions is not unidirectional; rather, people's views on location can significantly influence how the multilevel system itself is perceived and should be designed. This underscores the critical importance of location decisions in moulding the very framework of our society.

Moreover, when changes related to urbanisation or ageing populations challenge public service provision, decisions regarding service location become a means to address or mitigate demographic changes. However, taking a comprehensive approach and implementing structural reforms to tackle such challenges is difficult and fraught with risk. Structural reforms alter power relations between central and local levels of government, as well as between central and peripheral areas, and may jeopardise the legitimacy of institutions in the eyes of the public. Even reforms that seem necessary from a rational perspective and achieve their goals in maintaining high-quality services can provoke discontent. This underscores the importance of ensuring that the location decisions made within these multilevel systems are perceived as legitimate—and this leads us to the theme of the next two chapters, which will focus on the political and democratic perspectives on the location of services.

References

Axelsson, S. (2023). *Åsikt om vindkraft i Sverige 2022*. The SOM-institute, University of Gothenburg.

Axelsson, S., Matti, S., & Rönnerstrand, B. (2023). Fångad av en vindkraftsdebatt. In U. Andersson, P. Öhberg, A. Carlander, J. Martinsson, & N. Theorin (Eds.), *Ovisshetens tid*. The SOM-institute, University of Gothenburg.

Baldersheim, H., & Rose, L. E. (Eds.). (2010). *Territorial choice: The politics of boundaries and borders*. Palgrave Macmillan.

Bidwell, D. (2013). The role of values in public beliefs and attitudes towards commercial wind energy. *Energy Policy, 58*, 189–199.

Christaller, W. (1966). *Central places in southern Germany*. Prentice-Hall.

Cras, P. (2017). *Landsbygdssamhällets medborgarskap – en studie av organisering av service och infrastruktur i gränslandet mellan det ideella, kommersiella och politiska*. Doctoral dissertation, Swedish University of Agricultural Sciences.

Cras, P., Nordfeldt, M., Åberg, P., & von Essen, J. (2023). Kan civilsamhället lösa landsbygdernas serviceutmaningar? In S. Stenbacka & B. Hermelin (Eds.), *Hållbar samhällsplanering för landsbygden*. Gleerups Utbildning AB.

Dahl, R. A. (1989). *Democracy and its critics*. Yale University Press.

Dahl, R. A., & Tufte, E. (1973). *Size and democracy*. Stanford University Press.

de Fine Licht, J., Karlsson, D., & Skoog, L. (2023). Här, där eller överallt? Medborgares åsikter om lokalisering av offentlig service. In U. Andersson, P. Öhberg, A. Carlander, J. Martinsson, & N. Thorin (Eds.), *Ovisshetens tid*. The SOM-institute, University of Gothenburg.

Denters, B., Goldsmith, M., Ladner, A., Mouritzen, P. E., & Rose, L. E. (2014). *Size and local democracy*. Edward Elgar Publishing.

Dunleavy, P., Margetts, H., Bastow, S., & Tinkler, J. (2006). New public management is dead—long live digital-era governance. *Journal of Public Administration Research and Theory, 16*(3), 467–494.

Erlingsson, G. Ó., & Ödalen, J. (2017). A normative theory of local government: Connecting individual autonomy and local self-determination with democracy. *Lex Localis–Journal of Local Self-Government, 15*(2), 329–342.

Erlingsson, G. Ó., Öhrvall, R., Wallman Lundåsen, S., & Zerne, A. (2021). *Centrum mot periferi?: Om missnöje och framtidstro i Sveriges olika landsdelar* (version 2). Linköping University Electronic Press.

Erlingsson, G. Ó., Öhrvall, R., & Wallman Lundåsen, S. (2023). Geographical tensions within municipalities? Evidence from Swedish local governments. *Rural Sociology, 88*(4), 1033–1068.

Esping-Andersen, G. (1990). *The three worlds of welfare capitalism*. Polity.

Eythórsson, G. T., & Karlsson, V. (2018). The impact of amalgamations on services in Icelandic municipalities. *Nordicum – Mediterraneum, 13*, 1–18.

Forsberg, A. (2010). *Kamp för bygden – en etnologisk studie av lokalt utvecklingsarbete*. Doctoral dissertation, Umeå University.

Funck, E. K., & Karlsson, T. S. (2020). Twenty-five years of studying new public management in public administration: Accomplishments and limitations. *Financial Accountability and Management, 36*(4), 347–375.

Galizzi, G., Rota, S., & Sicilia, M. (2023). Local government amalgamations: State of the art and new ways forward. *Public Management Review*, 1–23.

Gendźwiłł, A., Kurniewicz, A., & Swianiewicz, P. (2021). The impact of municipal territorial reforms on the economic performance of local governments. A systematic review of quasi-experimental studies. *Space and Polity, 25*(1), 37–56.

Gilljam, M., Karlsson, D., & Sundell, A. (2010). *Politik på hemmaplan. Tiotusen fullmäktigeledamöter tycker om demokrati*. SKL Kommentus.

Hammarlund, C., & Nordin, M. (2023). *Saving countryside shops–Does government support increase survival and economic performance of grocery stores in rural Sweden?* AgriFood Economics Centre, Lund University.

Hansen, S. W., & Kjaer, U. (2020). Local territorial attachment in times of jurisdictional consolidation. *Political Geography, 83*, 102268.

Hansson-Forman, K., Reimerson, E., Bjärstig, T., & Sandström, C. (2021). A view through the lens of policy formulation: The struggle to formulate Swedish moose policy. *Journal of Environmental Policy and Planning, 23*(4), 528–542.

Harjunen, O., Saarimaa, T., & Tukiainen, J. (2021). Political representation and effects of municipal mergers. *Political Science Research and Methods, 9*(1), 72–88.

Hood, C. (1991). A public management for all seasons? *Public Administration, 69*(1), 3–19.

Hooghe, L., & Marks, G. (2003). Unraveling the central state, but how? Types of multi-level governance. *The American Political Science Review, 97*, 233–243.

Hysing, E. (2022). Designing collaborative governance that is fit for purpose: Theorising policy support and voluntary action for road safety in Sweden. *Journal of Public Policy, 42*(2), 201–223.

Jansson, M., Carlström, E., Karlsson, D., & Berlin, B. (2021). Drivers of outsourcing and backsourcing in the public sector—From idealism to pragmatism. *Financial Accountability and Management, 37*(3), 262–278.

Johansson, V., Lindgren, L., & Montin, S. (2018). *Den kommunala statliga ämbetsmannen*. Studentlitteratur.

Karlsson, D. (2013). A democracy of scale: Size and representative democracy in Swedish local government. *Scandinavian Journal of Public Administration, 17*(1), 7–28.

Karlsson, D. (2015). Local autonomy or national equality? A conflict of values and interests for political leaders. *Regional and Federal Studies, 25*(1), 19–44.

Karlsson, D. (2017). *Kommun- och landstingsfullmäktigeundersökningen (KOLFU)*. University of Gothenburg.

Karlsson, D. (Ed.). (2018). *Folkets främsta företrädare*. University of Gothenburg.

Karlsson, D. (2022a). Svenska politikers syn på kommunalt självstyre, likvärdighet och decentralisering av service. In B. P. Larsson (Ed.), *Självstyrelse – värd att värna?* Stockholm.

Karlsson, D. (2022b). Lokalisering av offentlig service – ideologi och egenintresse. In P. Öhberg, H. Oscarsson, & J. Ahlbom (Eds.), *Folkviljans förverkligare*. Göteborgs universitet.

Karlsson, D., & Gilljam, M. (Eds.). (2014). Svenska politiker. Om de folkvalda i riksdag, landsting och kommun.

Kullberg, L., Blomqvist, P., & Winblad, U. (2018). Market-orienting reforms in rural health care in Sweden: How can equity in access be preserved? *International Journal for Equity in Health, 17,* 1–14.

Lapuente, V., & Van de Walle, S. (2020). The effects of new public management on the quality of public services. *Governance, 33*(3), 461–475.

Larsson, E., & Hultqvist, E. (2018). Desirable places: Spatial representations and educational strategies in the inner city. *British Journal of Sociology of Education, 39*(5), 623–637.

Leach, S., & Copus, C. (2023). *The strange demise of the local in local government: Bigger is not better.* Palgrave Macmillan.

Lidén, G., & Nyhlén, J. (2023). The governance of policy integration and policy coordination through joined-up government: How subnational levels counteract siloism and fragmentation within Swedish migration policy. *Regulation and Governance*. Published online ahead of print.

Lidström, A. (2018). *Asymmetrisk ansvarsfördelning på kommunal nivå: Underlagsrapport till Kommunutredningen.* Fi 2017: 02.

Lidström, A. (2022). Den kommunala självstyrelsen – utmaningar och möjligheter. In B. P. Larsson (Ed.), *Självstyre – värd att värna?* Sveriges Kommuner och Regioner.

Lindberg, E. (2005). *Vad kan medborgarna göra? Fyra fallstudier av samarbetsformer för frivilliga insatser i äldreomsorg och väghållning.* Doctoral dissertation, Stockholm University.

Lindvall, D. (2023). Why municipalities reject wind power: A study on municipal acceptance and rejection of wind power instalments in Sweden. *Energy Policy, 180,* 113664.

Maltais, A., Rosenberg, J. H., Hultin, J., & Beckman, L. (2019). The demos and its critics. *The Review of Politics, 81*(3), 435–457.

Marks, G. (1993). Structural policy and multilevel governance in the EC. In A. W. Cafruny & G. G. Rosenthal (Eds.), *The state of the European community, Vol. 2. The Maastricht debates and beyond.* Lynne Rienner Publishers.

Marshall, J. N. (2007). Public sector relocation policies in the UK and Ireland. *European Planning Studies, 15*(5), 645–666.

Marshall, J. N., Bradley, D., Hodgson, C., Alderman, N., & Richardson, R. (2005). Relocation, relocation, relocation: Assessing the case for public sector dispersal. *Regional Studies, 39*(6), 767–787.

Nilsson, B., & Lundgren, A. S. (2015). Logics of rurality: Political rhetoric about the Swedish North. *Journal of Rural Studies, 37,* 85–95.

Niskanen, J., Anshelm, J., & Haikola, S. (2024). A multi-level discourse analysis of Swedish wind power resistance, 2009–2022. *Political Geography, 108*, 103017.

Öhberg, P., Oscarsson, H., & Ahlbom, J. (Eds.). (2022). *Folkviljans förverkligare*. University of Gothenburg.

Pollitt, C., & Bouckaert, G. (2017). *Public management reform: A comparative analysis-into the age of austerity*. Oxford University Press.

Salemink, K., Strijker, D., & Bosworth, G. (2017). The community reclaims control? Learning experiences from rural broadband initiatives in the Netherlands. *Sociologia Ruralis, 57*, 555–575.

Sellers, J. M., Lidström, A., & Bae, Y. (2020). *Multilevel democracy: How local institutions and civil society shape the modern state*. Cambridge University Press.

Skoog, L., & Svärd, O. (2023). Företagspolitiker – en systematisk granskning av forskning om styrelsearbete. *Nordisk Administrativt Tidsskrift, 100*(1).

Spehar, A., Hinnfors, J., & Bucken-Knapp, G. (2017). Passing the buck: The case of failing multilevel governance and vulnerable EU migrants in Sweden. *Nordic Journal of Migration Research, 7*(2), 114–123.

Strandh, V. (2023). *Hur kan service och trygghetspunkter (SOT) på landsbygden stärka lokalsamhällens krisberedskap och förmåga att hantera kriser?* Umeå Working Papers in Crisis Management Studies.

Svensson, P. (2019). Formalized policy entrepreneurship as a governance tool for policy integration. *International Journal of Public Administration, 42*(14), 1212–1221.

Swianiewicz, P. (2018). If territorial fragmentation is a problem, is amalgamation a solution? – Ten years later. *Local Government Studies, 44*(1), 1–10.

Swianiewicz, P., Gendźwiłł, A., & Zardi, A. (2017). Territorial reforms in Europe: Does size matter? *Territorial Amalgamation Toolkit: Centre of Expertise for Local Government Reform*. Council of Europe.

Syssner, J. (2020). *Pathways to demographic adaptation: Perspectives on policy and planning in depopulating areas in Northern Europe*. Springer Nature.

Tillväxtverket. (2021). *Tillgänglighet till kommersiell och offentlig service 2021*. Tillväxtverket.

Walker, C., Stephenson, L., & Baxter, J. (2018). "His main platform is 'stop the turbines'": Political discourse, partisanship and local responses to wind energy in Canada. *Energy Policy, 123*, 670–681.

Wolsink, M. (2000). Wind power and the NIMBY-myth: Institutional capacity and the limited significance of public support. *Renewable Energy, 21*(1), 49–64.

Wänström, J., & Persson, B. (2023). Local governments on an equal footing? Policy coordination between Swedish regions and municipalities in regional development policy. *Regional and Federal Studies*, 1–24.

CHAPTER 5

Party Conflicts and Political Representation

In Western democracies, the expectation is that the political decisions made by political representatives should reflect the will of the people. Difficult political trade-offs inherent to decisions on location of public services only gain legitimacy if the actors and institutions of representative democracy function as intended.

Deciding on physical locations for attractive services (LALU) involves choosing which groups of people—residing in different geographical areas—will benefit from high access to these services and which will not. Deciding where unwanted service facilities (LULU) are to be placed means prioritising which groups and geographical areas that will be spared from their presence—and which are not. Similarly, deciding whether a digital alternative is sufficient to ensure service quality or whether a private or non-profit organisation can fulfil welfare tasks that are otherwise a public responsibility means prioritising between values of efficiency and equality. While each decision is highly dependent on its context, these considerations are clearly connected to ideology and political visions for society as a whole. The outcome is likely to depend on the ideology of the elected political leaders and parties, particularly regarding questions such as: to what extent can citizens expect equal access to public services regardless of their place of residence? And to what extent can parts of the population be expected to carry burdens for the benefit of the majority?

© The Author(s), under exclusive license to Springer Nature Switzerland AG 2024
J. de Fine Licht et al., *Location of Public Services*, Palgrave Studies in Sub-National Governance,
https://doi.org/10.1007/978-3-031-64463-4_5

This chapter places the location dilemma in the domain of representative democracy. We start by discussing the role of political parties in channelling political conflicts on location decisions. Thereafter, we illustrate how they represent public opinion in location decisions using Swedish survey data as an example. As will become evident, there are numerous challenges for parties and representative democracy to overcome in making location decisions that resonate with the will of the people and thereby bestow legitimacy.

Party Conflicts Over Public Service Provision and Facility Location

In a vibrant democracy, the presence of ideological polarisation and conflicts over the allocation of services—both LALUs and LULUs—is essential. Meaningful and articulated differences between political alternatives are inherent in the very definition of democracy. Political parties have a fundamental role in articulating and representing the diverse opinions of the citizenry. The purpose of parties lies in their ability to aggregate and advocate for various political perspectives, facilitating a structured and institutionalised mechanism for decision-making. Polarisation has long been central to political science frameworks that study changes in party systems and competition between parties (e.g. Downs, 1957; Robertson, 1976; Sartori, 1976; Stokes, 1966). However, party conflicts and polarisation are not static; they vary over time and across different issues.

Some policy areas are often associated with a heightened conflict and party polarisation as they have been shaped around issues that reflect the societal cleavage structures that have laid the foundation for the emergence and development of the party system. Lipset and Rokkan argued that the party structure and lines of conflict between parties primarily reflect the societal structures that existed in the 1920s, shaped by societal cleavage structures that can trace back several hundred years (Lipset & Rokkan, 1967). As outlined in Chap. 2, we argue that the broader concept of the centre-periphery divide is of special importance for the politics of public service allocation. The number of places where services can be provided is always limited, and every political decision made by political representatives on allocation of service and infrastructure facilities becomes a balancing act between the interests of different groups living in central or peripheral geographical areas. There will inevitably be variations in proximity to LALUs and LULUs, with certain individuals residing further from the former and nearer to the latter. Hence, allocation of services, both LALUs and LULUs, can be seen as a territorial struggle for resources and power between geographically determined social groups, unfolding in the tension between central and peripheral regions.

This struggle can be expected to manifest in parliamentary arenas through political parties representing the positions of their voters. Parties' ideological foundation as expressed in their programmes are sometimes linked to support for groups who live in different places, or that groups who live in certain areas are more inclined to support specific parties (Gimpel et al., 2020; Johnston & Pattie, 2006; Rickardsson, 2021). Tensions, lines of conflict, and polarisation between centre-periphery can affect voters' party preference (Jacobs & Munis, 2023; Wallman Lundåsen & Erlingsson, 2023b), as well as the relationships between political parties (Skoog & Karlsson, 2018).

In classic models of representative democracy, multi-party systems, like in Sweden, are expected to be more ideologically polarised, with greater distance in political dissent between parties, than two-party systems. This is built on the idea that as multi-party systems allow for broader range of alternatives for voters to choose from, thus a wider range of political ideologies and perspectives among political parties is also to be expected. In contrast, two-party systems may exhibit a tendency towards convergence in the ideological space, as parties seek to capture the median voters, meaning that parties in a two-party system may moderate their positions to appeal to a broader spectrum of voters (Oscarsson et al., 2021). However, all is not so easy. For example, Sweden has a multi-party system and could theoretically be expected to have a higher degree of polarisation, yet Swedish politics has traditionally been described as consensus-oriented (e.g. Lewin, 2002; Lijphart, 1999). And countries having a majoritarian system where 'the winner takes all', for example the US, seems to introduce different dynamics where place and geographies have greater significance than in proportional systems, such as in many European countries including Sweden, and are often associated with a greater polarisation (Klein, 2020; Rodden, 2019). But recent comparative studies have indicated that while urban-rural divides have been more pronounced in the US, the UK, and Canada, these divides have now emerged in several

European multi-party systems as well (Huijsmans & Rodden, 2024). And lastly, polarisation between parties may be strong—even in situations where their positions on policies are close. For example, political actors may refuse to cooperate and instead strive to emphasise their differences, openly critique one another, and behave in a disrespectful manner with the goal of hindering opponents from exerting influence (Skoog, 2019). This may ultimately result in animosity and hostile feelings towards opponents, so-called affective polarisation (Iyengar & Westwood, 2015).

However, geography can still become a political issue in electoral systems that have multi-member constituencies that foster multi-party competition (Huijsmans & Rodden, 2024), even if the role of location in terms of constituencies is less significant than in two-party majority systems. In a multi-party setting, the centre-periphery divide is perhaps more likely to influence the formation of at least some of the parties when compared to a two-party system. Even though, there is of course nothing preventing parties in a two-party system from addressing this conflict dimension. Chapter 2 discusses how political sentiment, particularly in the centre-periphery divide, can shape the political discourse. How these conflicts are expressed varies between countries. Taking the case of Sweden as an example, where potential tensions exist between growing urban areas and sparsely populated, geographically extensive, and shrinking regions, there are noticeable differences in opinions between the population in the centre and the periphery. For instance, residents in rural areas tend to be somewhat less satisfied with public services, less satisfied with democracy at national level, and have a lower level of trust in public institutions (e.g. Öhrvall, 2023). However, recent studies indicate that there is no significant, and certainly no growing, polarisation of opinions between urban and rural areas in Sweden (Erlingsson et al., 2021; Larsson et al., 2020; Oscarsson et al., 2021). One notable trend that may be altering this situation is the rise of the anti-immigrant right-wing party, the Sweden Democrats (SD). Their success has been most pronounced outside urban areas and in regions with limited access to public services (Rickardsson, 2021; Wallman Lundåsen, 2024). If the conflict between the Sweden Democrats and centre-left parties, which is primarily associated with their positions on the GAL-TAN scale (Green-Alternative Libertarian vs. Traditional-Authoritarian, cf. Demker & Odmalm, 2022), begins to encompass the centre-periphery divide, it could lead to new patterns in the differences of opinion between urban and rural areas.

POLITICAL PARTIES AND LOCATION ISSUES

Even if an issue may be highly political, this does not mean that political parties politicise it. There may be several reasons for why political parties avoid party politicising certain issues. One reason could be that parties will, as long as possible, try to avoid making tough decisions by searching for alternative solutions. We will return to this issue in Chap. 6. Another reason could be that while political issues may not always be a topic of politicisation *between* parties, they could be subject to conflicts within or across parties (Giannetti & Benoit, 2008; Plescia et al., 2021). At times, established parties may fail to adapt to changing preferences of voters, which at best could lead to the establishment of new parties (Lawson & Merkl, 1988) and at worst could lead to a political vacuum and citizen frustration, potentially allowing political populists to become the dominant alternatives (Mair, 2013, p. 18ff; Mudde & Kaltwasser, 2017). Establishment of LULUs and removals of LALUs, such as closures of public indoor swimming pools (PISP) and hospital closures, are prime examples that show that location of services may have political consequences (e.g. Bolet, 2021; Isaksson, 2023). They may even provide fertile ground to create a local voter base for the establishment of a local or regional political party (e.g. Åberg & Ahlberger, 2015; Fridolfsson & Gidlund, 2002).

One striking example is the Swedish municipality of Herrljunga, where a local party named 'Municipal welfare' (Swedish: *Kommunens Väl*) was established in 2006 as citizens mobilised to oppose closure of a public indoor swimming pool (PISP) in one of the peripheral areas of the municipality. Remarkably, at its peak, the party gathered close to 30 per cent of the votes in the municipality and 65 per cent in the constituency where the threatened PISP was located—becoming the largest party in the local council. These achievement levels are unusually high for a local anti-establishment party in Sweden. Currently, the largest local party in Sweden is 'Independent Realists' (Swedish: *Oberoende Realister*) in Hagfors municipality. Their party programme and electoral pledges are focused on upholding a decentralised public service with great service accessibility in rural areas. In the 2022 election, the party received close to 42 per cent of the votes. At regional level, the largest party is 'the Healthcare party of Västernorrland' (Swedish: *Sjukvårdspartiet Västernorrland*); it was founded in the 1990s with the focus on saving a smaller hospital from closure. In the 2022 election, the party received 18 per cent of the votes in Västernorrland (Swedish Electoral Authority).

In the Deep End—Public Indoor Swimming Pools as a LALU Challenge

There are over 400 public indoor swimming pools (PISP) in Sweden. Most were built in the 1960s and 1970s during the expansion of the welfare state, driven in part by a political emphasis on public health and swimming skills (which is much needed in a country of lakes and long coastlines). A PISP often also functions as a hub for a local community. But as the expected durability of a swimming pool is 30–50 years, many are now at the end of their rope. Estimations indicate that about three-fourth of them are in dire need of costly renovations (Kejerhag, 2023).

For citizens, closing a PISP means loss of a venue for socialisation and health-promotion, and that school children must take a longer bus ride to practise their swimming skills. But while they are greatly appreciated, a swimming pool is not necessary for a good life. And in a situation where hard prioritisations must be made, most people would likely choose to uphold a school instead of a PISP. But the choice is rarely that simple.

Municipality 'M' in northern Sweden represents a typical case of how practical concerns are intertwined with symbolism in location decisions. M is geographically large, even more so than three EU member states—Cyprus, Luxembourg, and Malta. Simultaneously, it is very sparsely populated and has a declining population. Half of the population lives in the central town, while the other half is scattered throughout the municipality in villages. In total, M has three PISPs and three heated public outdoor pools. By all comparisons, this is a lot to carry for an already strained municipal budget. The general narrative is that the PISPs in M were built just before the last municipal amalgamation reform in Sweden, where the 'old' municipalities emptied their budgets and built a PISP in their respective central settlements. This is described as a form of symbolic resistance towards the reform that was forced on them from 'above'. Several of M's PISPs are now over 50 years old. For one of them, discussion about a potential closure has been ongoing since the early 1980s.

The financially logical solution would likely be to close several pools and direct funds to other policy areas, but the prospects of gaining public acceptance to do so are perceived as low. As the chair of the executive board, the Swedish mayor equivalent, puts it in an interview with us:

(continued)

> (continued)
>
> We often joke about it in local council circles, that it's probably one of the most sensitive things you can deal with. Those damn swimming pools, you know.
>
> Experiences from earlier attempts to speak openly about the problem are not positive. Once, the political majority of M initiated a proposal to close a PISP in one of the villages. This resulted in a heated public meeting and with the politicians withdrawing the proposal and instructing the Director of recreation and leisure activities to, with the little resources that could be spared, 'patch and mend' to keep it functional for a few more years. But as the chief of executive operations (CEO) summarises it in an interview with us:
>
>> So, it's about how responsible politicians we have. Essentially. And being prepared for the consequences. Because if we choose to invest in multiple recreational facilities and we have a fixed amount of money to allocate, then there is less for healthcare. Less for schools. That's the consequence. This must be understood.
>
> The municipal administration has at times indicated towards the political leadership that one of the swimming pools is in poor condition. But the public uproar if a PISP is closed is perceived as too great, and the message from the political leaders is that the pool must be kept open as long as possible. Thereby, the PISPs illustrate not only the centre-periphery divide for location issues but also the difference between political and administrative logics.

Local parties may certainly contribute to democracy by strengthening grassroots participation and engaging citizens in political processes and decisions. When the public feel that their voices and opinions have a direct impact on local issues, and when conflicts in a polity are channelled into democratic processes, this might serve to strengthen legitimacy for local political institutions, especially when people feel that the established parties fail to channel their concerns in these matters. However, local parties are at times known for oversimplifying complex problems and offering emotionally charged solutions that lack nuance. They may frame issues in an 'us versus them'-manner, creating heated debates within the community. Studies also show that when local parties are present in municipal councils, the general level of political conflict is heightened (Skoog & Karlsson, 2018) and their voters have been referred to as being 'anti-establishment' (Wallman Lundåsen & Erlingsson, 2023a). Research also indicates that there is an urban versus rural divide in the success of so-called radical right-wing parties, where they tend to drum up more supporters in rural areas (De Lange & Rooduijn, 2015; Fitzgerald, 2018) and that this may be linked to variations in public service supply (Cremaschi et al., 2023; Nyholt, 2023; Rickardsson, 2021; Wallman Lundåsen, 2024), indicating that such sentiments are not evenly distributed across a territory. To be clear, not all local parties exhibit populistic, anti-establishment, or radical right-wing characteristics. But there is an intersection between populism and localism (Chou et al., 2022)—that at times is nourished by service closures.

How Do Parties Represent the Opinions of Citizens in Location Issues?

From the preceding section, it is evident that political issues related to the location of public services or the centre-periphery divide, in a broader sense, can exhibit varying degrees of party polarisation. This variation depends, among other factors, on how conflicting interests manifest themselves and on the composition of the party system. In a well-functioning representative democracy, the legitimacy of the system hinges on the ability of elected representatives to make decisions that align with the will of the public. When the positions held by elected representatives reflect the concerns and issues that are significant to the public, it establishes a direct link between the electorate and the decision-making process. This connection is fundamental to upholding the democratic principle of representation, where leaders are entrusted to advocate for and enact policies that resonate with the needs and values of their constituents.

The mechanism expected to facilitate this alignment of views between voters and the elected in a party-based democracy is that groups of voters with differing opinions should have the opportunity to identify parties that share their views, that is the collective policy congruence is strong (Holmberg, 1999). Ideally, each group finds a party to vote for, and the distribution of opinions among the population mirrors exactly in the elected assembly. However, if the issue in question—in this case, location policy—is not politicised along party lines, it becomes challenging to discern differences between parties, leading to a breakdown in the mechanism. Moreover, if voters' party choices do not appear to align with their views on service location, then there are no grounds to use election results as an indicator of public opinion on these matters.

But to what extent do political representatives truly represent the opinions of citizens regarding the location of services? In this chapter, we have the opportunity to make such comparisons based on data from the Swedish case. These results, which we believe are unique in the literature on location, are published for the first time in this book. Even though the findings are specifically related to the Swedish context, they nonetheless clearly illuminate how the issue of policy congruence in location issues can be analysed and interpreted.

In Chap. 2, we presented results concerning public opinion on these matters. Additionally, a couple of questions posed in citizen surveys have also been included in surveys directed at politicians on all tiers of government (Karlsson, 2022). One of the questions was intended to capture the ideological dimension relating to spatial allocation of services, referred to as the c/d-scale, and another concerned the willingness to preserve schools in small villages and rural areas. This affords us the opportunity to make direct comparisons of the congruence, both between the electorate and their representatives in general (Fig. 5.1), and between supporters of specific parties and the views held by their elected representatives from those parties (Fig. 5.2).

In Fig. 5.1, there is a notable congruence on the c/d-scale between citizens and politicians across all levels. The most common response is the neutral midpoint (5), which may be expected in complex issues where many feel some uncertainty in taking a stance. It is not surprising that citizens exhibit a higher proportion of neutral responses than politicians on such a question, as politicians are typically more accustomed to addressing complex issues. Additionally, across all categories, there is a tendency towards preferring decentralisation over centralisation, with politicians consistently appearing to be marginally more in favour of decentralisation than citizens. Amongst the politicians, national MPs are more in favour of decentralisation compared to their municipal and regional counterparts. The mean value across all groups lies between 6.1 and 6.3 and does not differ in a statistically significant way. The primary outcome of this inquiry,

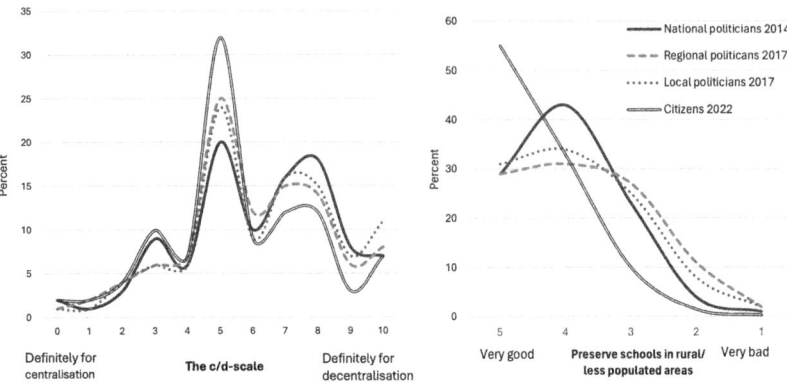

Fig. 5.1 Distribution of responses to questions on spatial allocation of services (the c/d-scale) and support for preserving schools in small villages and rural areas among citizens and politicians at national, regional, and local levels (percentage). (Sources: National politicians: the RDU survey 2014 N = 265 (Karlsson & Lindstrand, 2018); regional politicians (N = 1074) and local politicians (N = 7444) from the KOLFU survey 2017 (Karlsson, 2017); citizens (N = 1674) from The National SOM survey 2022 (de Fine Licht et al., 2023). *Note*: The figure illustrates the distribution of responses for two survey questions. The first question related to the c/d-scale was: 'Regarding the location of services, there is sometimes talk of a political dimension between: Those who want centralised public services (for the sake of efficiency and quality), and those who want decentralised public services (to promote equitable access to services everywhere). Where would you personally place yourself on a centralisation-decentralisation scale?' The responses were given on a 0–10 scale from definitely for centralisation to definitely for decentralisation. The second question was presented as a proposal 'Preserve schools in rural/less populated areas' and the responses were given on a scale from 1 'very bad' to 5 'very good' proposal)

therefore, suggests that both the spread and the mean values indicate an extremely accurate reflection of opinions between voters and their elected representatives.

Regarding the issue of preserving schools in rural areas, there is also a notable level of congruence, with a substantial majority of both citizens and politicians at all levels advocating for the decentralist position. However, citizens are markedly more decentralist, while politicians, as a group, show a broader spectrum of opinions. MPs are the most decentralist, whereas local and regional politicians count a higher number of centralists among them.

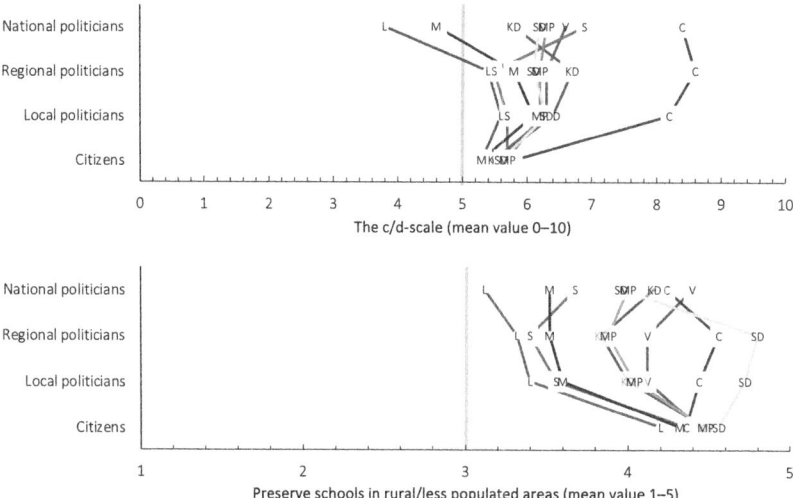

Fig. 5.2 Policy congruence between citizens and politicians by party affiliation regarding spatial allocation of services (the c/d-scale) and support for preserving schools in small villages and rural areas (mean values). (*Note*: For the formulation of survey questions and sources for the three surveys, refer to the note on Fig. 5.1. In this figure, responses are represented as mean values on the c/d scale (0 representing definitely for centralisation, 10 representing definitely for decentralisation) and the question regarding preserving schools (1 being a very bad proposal, 5 being a very good proposal), with a grey vertical line indicating the neutral position on each scale. Values are categorised according to party affiliation for the eight national parties (*L* Liberals, *M* Moderates [conservative], *KD* Christian Democrats, *SD* Sweden Democrats [nationalists], *MP* Greens, *V* Left Party [socialists], *S* Social Democrats, *C* Centre Party [agrarians]))

With this relatively high level of policy congruence between voters and elected representatives, one might expect that the party system effectively captures the differences in opinions on these two issues, offering their respective sympathisers among the electorate a means to channel their views into governing assemblies. However, when dissecting the results by party sympathy among citizens and politicians at different levels, as illustrated in Fig. 5.2, a somewhat different picture emerges.

Indeed, the findings in Fig. 5.2 suggest there are some party differences on these matters among politicians across all political levels, potentially facilitating such a democratic mechanism through elections.

On the c/d-scale, there is a distinct decentralist outlier: the Centre Party (C). Initially founded as the 'Farmers' Union', this party has long championed rural interests and is particularly influenced by the centre-periphery divide. The somewhat paradoxical name of the Centre Party, associated with the geographical periphery, in this case stems from the party's historical centrality on the left-right political spectrum and bears no reference to geography. However, it is noteworthy that at local and regional levels, the Sweden Democrats (SD) tends to be more decentralist than the Centre Party in the issue of preserving schools in rural areas. The most unequivocally centralist party on both issues is the Liberals (L), whose primary voter base is in urban areas, both historically and currently. It is interesting to observe that the Centre Party and the Liberals, usually close allies on many fronts, are diametrically opposed on this issue.

Nonetheless, in these two location-based issues, party affiliation does not explain variations in politicians' opinions as effectively as it does in other areas, such as opinions on political issues related to the left-right spectrum. For example, only two parties at the national level (the Liberals and the Moderates) have representatives slightly inclined towards centralisation on the c/d-scale, with all other parties leaning towards decentralisation. Regarding preservation of schools in rural areas, no party group at any level advocates a centralist stance. This suggests that there is potential for improvement if parties were to strive for greater internal cohesion, thus offering more distinct choices in elections.

The most striking result in Fig. 5.2, however, concerns the positions of citizens. Regarding the c/d-scale, it is difficult to identify any statistically significant differences in opinions between citizens with different party affiliations. The differences are marginally more pronounced in the issue on preserving rural schools, where we observe a reflection of the degree of sympathy for decentralism that corresponds to politicians of their party of choice. The unavoidable conclusion from these observations is that the party choices of voters scarcely mirror their views on location politics.

This exploration of the issue of collective policy congruence between voters and elected officials in the case of Sweden paints a somewhat contradictory picture. On the one hand, there is a generally strong agreement in opinions on the two issues, both in terms of the mean values and the spread among the groups of citizens and politicians. However, on the other hand, this congruence does not stem from party choice in elections. The differences in opinions on these issues are more pronounced within parties than between them, particularly among voters. This suggests that if Swedish voters want to use their ballots to influence location-specific issues—which they currently seem not to do—finding a suitable party is not straightforward. This is especially true for the relatively large minority with a centralist stance on the c/d-scale, where the options are few.

The results regarding policy congruence cannot, of course, easily be generalised to other countries, where the issues and party system may look completely different. However, our deep dive into the Swedish case on these matters illustrates how the problematic can be understood and what questions need to be asked to check if representative democracy is capable of handling location issues.

Summary

As we have seen in this chapter, political institutions and actors of representative democracy struggle to address the issues of service location in various ways. It is by no means a given that even a well-functioning democratic system can manage these issues as well as they deserve. The challenges are particularly significant for political parties. The formation of local parties that have positions on location issues that established parties have failed to represent can be interpreted as a sign of vitality, but such local parties are often perceived as problematic for other reasons.

Another pressing concern for political parties is the palpable decline for membership that underscores a disconnection between citizens and political representatives. The traditional party structures now struggle with a diminished capacity to capture the opinions and experiences of an increasingly diverse and dynamic society (Erlingsson et al., 2022). This means that simultaneously as political parties and their representatives struggle with declining party membership and an increasing gap between them and their voters, they must also make decisions on location of services that risk upsetting the population. This casts doubt over their ability to reflect their voters' opinions but also of their ability to communicate their decisions and convince citizens of the need to make tough decisions such as reducing services in peripheral areas.

Additionally, the ascent of populist movements has introduced a disruptive element to the conventional party-political paradigm. The allure of populistic and anti-establishment parties poses great challenges for established political parties. But as Mouffe (2011) argues, democratic institutions and political parties must counter this development by openly displaying social tensions and political conflicts within the political institutions—not hide uncomfortable decisions. And how such decisions can be made in a legitimate manner is the theme for the next chapter.

References

Åberg, M., & Ahlberger, C. (2015). Local candidate lists: Historical artefacts or a novel phenomenon? A research note. *Party Politics, 21*(5), 813–820.

Bolet, D. (2021). Drinking alone: Local socio-cultural degradation and radical right support – The case of British pub closures. *Comparative Political Studies, 54*(9), 1653–1692.

Chou, M., Moffitt, B., & Busbridge, R. (2022). The localist turn in populism studies. *Swiss Political Science Review, 28*(1), 129–141.

Cremaschi, S., Rett, P., Cappelluti, M., & De Vries, C. E. (2023). *Geographies of discontent: Public Service deprivation and the rise of the far right in Italy.* Harvard Business School.

de Fine Licht, J., Karlsson, D., & Skoog, L. (2023). Här, där eller överallt? Medborgares åsikter om lokalisering av offentlig service. In U. Andersson, P. Öhberg, A. Carlander, J. Martinsson, & N. Thorin (Eds.), *Ovisshetens tid*. The SOM-institute, University of Gothenburg.

De Lange, S. L., & Rooduijn, M. (2015). Contemporary populism, the Agrarian and the rural in Central Eastern and Western Europe. In D. Strijker, G. Voerman, & I. J. Terluin (Eds.), *Rural protest groups and populist political parties* (pp. 163–190). Wageningen Academic Publishers.

Demker, M., & Odmalm, P. (2022). From governmental success to governmental breakdown: How a new dimension of conflict tore apart the politics of migration of the Swedish centre-right. *Journal of Ethnic and Migration Studies, 48*(2), 425–440.

Downs, A. (1957). *An economic theory of democracy*. Harper.

Erlingsson, G. Ó., Isaksson, Z., & Persson, B. (2021). *Mellankommunal samverkan: vad är känt om dess effekter? En inventering av kunskapsläget*. Kommuninvest.

Erlingsson, G., Karlsson, D., Wide, J., & Öhrvall, R. (2022). *Demokratirådets rapport 2022: Den lokala demokratins vägval*. SNS.

Fitzgerald, J. (2018). *Close to home: Local ties and voting radical right in Europe*. Cambridge University Press.

Fridolfsson, C., & Gidlund, G. (2002). *De lokala partierna och den nya politiska kartan*. Novemus, Örebro universitet.

Giannetti, D., & Benoit, K. (Eds.). (2008). *Intra-party politics and coalition governments*. Routledge.

Gimpel, J. G., Lovin, N., Moy, B., & Reeves, A. (2020). The urban–rural gulf in American political behavior. *Political Behavior, 42,* 1343–1368.
Holmberg, S. (1999). Collective policy congruence compared. In W. Miller et al. (Eds.), *Policy representation in western democracies* (pp. 87–109). Oxford University Press.
Huijsmans, T., & Rodden, J. (2024). The great global divider? A comparison of urban-rural partisan polarization in western democracies. *Comparative Political Studies,* 00104140241237458.
Isaksson, Z. (2023). The political effects of rural school closures – Evidence from Sweden. *Journal of Rural Studies, 100,* 103009.
Iyengar, S., & Westwood, S. J. (2015). Fear and loathing across party lines: New evidence on group polarization. *American Journal of Political Science, 59*(3), 690–707.
Jacobs, N., & Munis, B. K. (2023). Place-based resentment in contemporary US elections: The individual sources of America's urban-rural divide. *Political Research Quarterly, 76*(3), 1102–1118.
Johnston, R., & Pattie, C. (2006). *Putting voters in their place: Geography and elections in Great Britain.* Oxford University Press.
Karlsson, D. (2017). *Kommun- och landstingsfullmäktigeundersökningen (KOLFU) 2017.* School of Public Administration, University of Gothenburg.
Karlsson, D. (2022). Svenska politikers syn på kommunalt självstyre, likvärdighet och decentralisering av service. In B. P. Larsson (Ed.), *Självstyrelse – värd att värna?* Sveriges Kommuner och Regioner.
Karlsson, D., & Lindstrand, L. (2018). Om riksdagsundersökningen. In D. Karlsson (Ed.), *Folkets främsta företrädare.* University of Gothenburg.
Kejerhag, J. (2023). Badhusräkning i Kiruna skenar – över 1 miljard. *Dagens Nyheter,* 2023-11-03.
Klein, E. (2020). *Why we're polarized.* Simon and Schuster.
Larsson, Y., Hedberg, P., & Holmberg, S. (2020). *Ökad polarisering mellan landsbygd och storstad?* Valforskningsprogrammets arbetsrapportserie, 2020 (4). University of Gothenburg.
Lawson, K., & Merkl, P. H. (Eds.). (1988). *When parties fail.* Princeton University Press.
Lewin, L. (2002). *Bråka inte! O vår tids demokratisyn.*
Lijphart, A. (1999). *Patterns of democracy: Government forms and performance in thirty-six countries.* Yale University Press.
Lipset, S. M., & Rokkan, S. (1967). Cleavage structures, party systems, and voter alignments: An introduction. In S. M. Lipset & S. Rokkan (Eds.), *Party systems and voter alignments* (pp. 1–64). Free Press.
Mair, P. (2013). *Ruling the void: The hollowing of western democracy.* Verso.
Mouffe, C. (2011). *On the political.* Routledge.
Mudde, C., & Kaltwasser, C. R. (2017). *Populism.* Oxford University Press.

Nyholt, N. (2023). Left behind: Voters' reactions to local school and hospital closures. *European Journal of Political Research*. Published online ahead of print.

Öhrvall, R. (2023). *Ett delat Sverige?: Om skillnader i livsvillkor, värderingar och åsikter mellan stad och land*. Centre for Local Government Studies, Linköping University.

Oscarsson, H., Bergman, T., Bergström, A., & Hellström, J. (2021). *Demokratirådets rapport 2021: Polariseringen i Sverige*. SNS förlag.

Plescia, C., Kritzinger, S., & Eberl, J. M. (2021). 'The enemy within': Campaign attention and motivated reasoning in voter perceptions of intra-party conflict. *Party Politics, 27*(5), 917–927.

Rickardsson, J. (2021). The urban–rural divide in radical right populist support: The role of resident's characteristics, urbanization trends and public service supply. *The Annals of Regional Science, 67*(1), 211–242.

Robertson, D. (1976). *A theory of party competition*. John Wiley.

Rodden, J. A. (2019). *Why cities lose: The deep roots of the urban-rural political divide*. Basic Books.

Sartori, G. (1976). *Parties and party systems: A framework for analysis*. Cambridge University Press.

Skoog, L. (2019). *Political conflicts: Dissent and antagonism among political parties in local government*. Doctoral dissertation, University of Gothenburg.

Skoog, L., & Karlsson, D. (2018). Causes of party conflicts in local politics. *Politics, 38*(2), 182–196.

Stokes, D. E. (1966). Spatial models of party competition. In A. Campbell, P. E. Converse, W. E. Miller, & D. E. Stokes (Eds.), *Elections and the political order*. John Wiley.

Wallman Lundåsen, S. (2024). Rurality and discontent: Unraveling the context effects of living in rural districts in local elections on support for Sweden Democrats. *Journal of Rural Studies, 106*, 103209.

Wallman Lundåsen, S., & Erlingsson, G. Ó. (2023a). The local party voter: A localist anti-establishment voter? *Electoral Studies, 82*, 102592.

Wallman Lundåsen, S., & Erlingsson, G. Ó. (2023b). Perceived fairness of intra-municipal cohesion politics: Does place of residence affect party preferences? *Political Geography, 107*, 102994.

CHAPTER 6

Making Decisions on Location

In a democratic system, the legitimacy of political decisions is built on whether they align with the will of the people. However, as we saw in the previous chapter, it is not always straightforward to interpret election results as a governance signal. Furthermore, once an election is over, political conflicts are to be handled in the everyday work of the political assembly. Regardless of whether the future of a public indoor swimming pool, for example, was a topic in a local election campaign or not, the question has now moved into the field of politico-administrative decision-making. How internal processes are organised is a balance between ideological, legal-administrative, and pragmatic considerations, which varies considerably between countries as well as across municipalities, or even between policy issues within the same municipality.

In this chapter, we address the issue of how political actors manage location issues and decisions. First, we discuss efforts to avoid making painful decisions by searching for alternatives, by delegating the problem to other actors, or by delaying the process. Thereafter, we introduce the difference between a decision-making model based on conflict where the winning side decides and a model based on compromise between stakeholders, and discuss which effects we can expect for transparency and accountability. Finally, we discuss the prospects of public involvement as a means to generate legitimacy for location decisions.

Avoiding Painful Decisions

As indicated in Chap. 5, it is not always the case that location issues are politicised at all. Political actors may be unwilling to engage in a debate about location of both wanted and unwanted service facilities and may instead attempt to avoid making painful decisions at all. An obvious reason is that decisions on location are often controversial and political actors may see no good coming from a debate that will upset substantial shares of the population—which for political parties represent their future voters. For some parties, especially smaller ones at the ends of the political spectrum, location controversies can indeed represent an opportunity to win votes. Many may, however, conclude that they have more to win by avoiding *blame* (Weaver, 1986) for controversial closures or placements, and may therefore avoid making decisions as long as possible.

There are three main alternatives for actors who do not want to make explicit decisions on locations: try to solve the problem without making a painful decision, try to delegate the decision to someone else, or try to delay the (eventually necessary) decision.

The first option is clearly the more attractive one and is often the first strategy used by actors who hesitate to make a controversial decision. For example, technical innovations can give rise to creative solutions when it comes to providing welfare services. By offering digital appointments to doctors or public servants, remote teaching in some subjects for children, or even use drones to deliver library books, politicians can claim that they are not shutting down welfare services in peripheral areas, but rather make them *more* accessible. Similarly, there are many hopes that typical LULUs such as energy plants will be smaller, quieter, and less visible, through innovative technical solutions, thereby reducing potential criticism. A related strategy that has become increasingly popular in times of welfare retrenchment is to engage private or civil society actors in service provision. For instance, parents in smaller villages in scarcely populated parts of Sweden have taken over the running of schools in cooperative form. Other examples are local sports associations managing nature and leisure areas, or volunteers organising activities for children or the elderly.

In some cases, strategies to find alternative solutions prove to be a successful approach and the need for painful prioritisations disappears. In many cases, however, the problem remains or reappears. Digital solutions may, for instance, serve some parts of the population well, while others may not buy the argument that they represent proper substitutes to face-to-face service. Some forms of services or goods provision simply demand a facility, for example a swimming pool. Similarly, delegating public tasks to passionate volunteers is economically appealing but raises concerns about operation quality, accountability, and user relationships, potentially becoming contentious. Civil society engagement may work smoothly until some significant enthusiasts quit.

When all ways of solving the problem are exhausted, political decision-makers may still try to avoid making painful decisions, such as deciding on the actual site of a LULU, by attempting to delegate the decision to someone else. A fairly common strategy is, for example, that politicians adopt loosely formulated policies to which everyone can agree and then handing it over to administrators and/or expert advisors to find solutions—hoping that the problem will go away (Skoog & Svensson, 2023). A related strategy is to blame outside actors. For example, if it appears too controversial to close a village school, politicians can quietly agree on waiting for the public audit organisation, in this case *the Swedish Schools Inspectorate*, to provide such severe criticism that a closing appears unavoidable, thereby shifting focus—and blame—from municipal to national level.

Finally, even if there is a shared understanding among the political actors that something needs to be done in a sensitive location matter, they may still try to delay the process of having to make a decision. For example, one can postpone a necessary closure of a valued facility by patching and mending as long as possible. Similarly, one can let investigations of proper sites for unwanted facilities take more time than absolutely needed to, for instance, avoid making an unpopular decision just before a political election.

However creative the decision-makers are, they will not be able to completely avoid difficult location decisions for more than a limited time. At some point, potentially painful decisions will have to be made.

Conflict or Compromise: Two Models of Democracy

When a location decision actually is to be made, there are differing views among scholars of democracy and political behaviour on how political conflicts are to be handled. In essence, should politicians strive to reach consensus or at least a functioning compromise in sensitive issues, or should they attempt to accentuate their differences and let the strongest part win? Although political and electoral systems may favour one model of democracy over the other, democratic actors across societal levels often have the autonomy to select their decision-making strategy. Hence, it's essential to discuss the implications of different democracy models for legitimacy in the context of location decisions.

A common distinction is between the majoritarian and consensual models of democracy. The majoritarian model, cantered on majority rule and competition, prioritises accountability. This approach, exemplified by Dahl (1989), underscores the need for an active opposition that openly exhibits differences between political parties. Contrastingly, the consensual model, advocated by Arend Lijphart (1999), opposes the monopolisation of political power by a majority. While recognising majority rule, its objective is to broaden the majority for widespread participation.

The two models of democracy have different consequences for how conflicts can be resolved. While the majoritarian model accentuates power concentration, ensuring responsiveness to the majority, the consensual model emphasises power division, fostering compromise and cross-party collaboration to mitigate differences. Majoritarian democracy prefers excluding the opposition from decision-making, promoting an active opposition, but openly embracing conflicts for public scrutiny. In contrast, the consensual model prioritises conflict resolution through compromises, aligning with its emphasis on power division and negotiation between majorities and minorities.

From a normative and democratic point of view, both models have pros and cons. Application of majority rule means that prioritising preferences of the majority at the expense of the minority, underscoring the risk of the 'tyranny of the majority'. If the majority of the population in a municipality lives in the major city, this may, for example, imply that the interests of the villages on the countryside will be downplayed when parties try to satisfy their voters. Similarly, if the majority lives in villages in rural areas, the result could also be a strong prioritisation of the countryside. On a positive note, the efficiency of majority rule allows for swift decision-making, which is crucial for effective governance. Simply put, it ensures that decisions align with the needs and preferences of the larger population. In the case of a proposed costly renovation of a public in-door swimming pool in the periphery, the majority of the population would perhaps prioritise other initiatives that benefit a larger number of individuals, thus reflecting broader societal priorities. Moreover, it is very clear who is responsible for a decision, which can help dissatisfied citizens to demand accountability in the next election.

If a more consensual model is applied, parties often seek mutual ground and try to come up with a final decision that as many as possible can agree on. Through compromises and negotiations, a 'giving and taking', the political parties—or at least a large share of the parties—can make a joint decision that they all can defend in relation to the public. The results of the negotiations can, of course, be a compromise that is to be the best for the community as a whole. Alternatively, it can be a decision that no one is really satisfied with. The benefit of a consensual approach is a lower risk for tyranny of the majority. Minority interests and opinions will be included, albeit to a lesser extent. Further, citizens generally value compromises, and at least in theory they expect politicians to be able to solve disagreements and deliver policy outcomes (e.g. Wolak, 2020). There are also good prospects for the decision to be stable, as the opposition is less likely to repeal a decision that they were a part of if they are more successful in the next election. Instead, as many—or all—political representatives support a decision, they can speak with one voice and explain to the public why they have chosen a particular alternative and how they plan to implement it. At best, this can generate confidence and legitimacy also among those on the losing side. On the other hand, when there is only one voice, it is less clear who is really responsible for the decision. For a dissatisfied citizen, it is difficult to demand accountability—and vote for politicians representing an opposing opinion—in the next election, potentially resulting in resentment in relation to the democratic system.

In practice, decision-makers often need to strike a balance between these ideals, where the level of conflictual debate, pragmatic bargaining, or constructive compromise varies not only between political settings but also depending on the hotness of a particular issue or the personal chemistry between individuals.

Open or Closed Decision-Making

Whether political actors primarily strive for winning or compromise may have consequences for the transparency of decision-making. The question of whether location decisions gain enhanced legitimacy through a more open decision-making process, however, is multifaceted.

Liberal democracy tends to hold a normative presumption in favour of transparency in political decision-making (e.g. Chambers, 2004). This speaks in favour of a vivid open debate which clarifies different standpoints and arguments and shows which representatives or parties that are on which sides. In contrast, in-house 'secret' decision-making is traditionally associated with dubious activities or even outright corruption, not least at local level (Bergh et al., 2017; Broms et al., 2019; Erlingsson et al., 2008; Wittberg, 2023).

At the same time, there is widespread recognition among researchers as well as practitioners that some issues—especially those that are complex, are technical, and involve multiple concerns to balance—might benefit from deliberation or negotiation in a comparatively private setting (e.g.

Chambers, 2004; Mansbridge, 2009; Warren & Mansbridge, 2013; de Fine Licht, 2020; Mokrosinska, 2023). This is true for many situations where representatives from different parties seek to come to an agreement on how to handle a difficult location decision. Behind closed doors, it might be easier for political actors to ask 'stupid' questions, try to see things from a new perspective, or even change their mind. In front of an audience, whether physically present or in the form of media, political actors may simply be too incentivised to catch potential votes in the next election to agree on the establishment of a LULU—or removal of a LALU—even if they think it would be the best for the community. This means that important decisions might be seriously delayed if debated in public.

Empirical studies show that settings for political debate that are kept from the public can foster more efficient and constructive discussions on problem-solving and policy alternatives. For example, Steiner et al. (2004) found in their extensive analysis of parliamentary debates that closed sessions can bring mutual understanding and respect between decision-makers on different sides. Similarly, Leirset (2021) shows in his comparison of the relatively closed meetings in local government settings in Denmark and the comparatively open meetings in Norway that closed meetings made politicians more able to deliberate in an open and willing-to-change-in-light-of-good-arguments manner. This means that faced by difficult and sensitive issues like potential location decisions, decision-makers may—for both theoretical and experience-based reasons—prefer a more internal process that restricts public involvement. In, for example, a situation where a closure of a valued public service facility might be necessary, politicians from the larger parties may want to have informal pre-meetings to discuss and explore potential common grounds and perhaps agree on a road map for the way forward—before the topic hits the headlines. Importantly, this may not necessarily be because they want to engage in dubious activities but because they see a need to come to agreement on how to handle a pressing issue for the better of their community.

The question of how transparent political decision-making should be is therefore not as easy as it might seem. Transparency demonstrates accountability and clearly increases the chances of procedural legitimacy. In the long run, open communication about the rationale behind decisions can also foster a more informed citizenry. On the other hand, decision-making in private settings might increase the chances of delivering actual results, that is legitimacy in terms of substance. Decision-makers have to navigate between these aspects in their everyday work.

Public Involvement in Decision-Making

That a policy issue is formally handled by the politico-administrative system does not mean that the public is a passive actor. This is especially true when location decisions are on the table. Typically, location decision about both LALUs and LULUs generate strong interest and engagement among the public and often result in various attempts to influence decision-making processes. Activities can range from personal contacts with politicians, petitioning, letter writing in media, conducting counter studies, and internet activism, to demonstrations, strikes, occupation of public buildings, or even (uninvited) visits to politicians' homes (e.g. Uba, 2016). While the former forms of participation are often welcomed by politicians and public officials as normal forms of citizen engagement in a healthy democracy as well as valuable sources of information (e.g. Hendriks & Lees-Marshment, 2019), the latter forms can be devastating both for society and individuals in governing positions. How to navigate public interest, influence, and activism is therefore a delicate concern for both political representatives and administrators.

In some cases, citizens are formally invited to participate in political decision-making. This can be a result of formal consultations demanded by law. For example, it is mandatory in Sweden to invite affected members of the public to consultations (Swedish: *samråd*) on issues related to plans for housing and land use, such as wind farm or solar power establishments. In addition, the indigenous population of Sweden, the Sámi people, has specific judicial rights to be consulted on matters impacting them and their lands. These kinds of mandatory hearings are often critiqued of not constituting 'real participation'. In terms of Sherry Arnstein's (1969) widely used 'ladder of citizen participation'—which rises from mere therapeutic or manipulative talk via information and various forms of consultative dialogues to decision-making in partnership and at the end total citizen control—public hearings are generally placed at a fairly low stage as it does not require actual influence.

In other cases, public authorities can choose to organise forums for discussion with citizens—as individuals or as organised interests—either as a one-time event or as a part of a more long-term strategy. At least rhetorically, these kinds of arrangements often have the ambition to reach higher up on the ladder and to involve a two-way dialogue or a possibility for citizens to provide recommendations. This way of engaging the public in decision-making has become increasingly popular in recent decades (Fung, 2015), both in academic exercises and in practical policymaking (e.g.

OECD, 2020). Policymakers' motives for introducing forums for public participation can, however, vary considerably. Clearly, some politicians are ideologically attracted to more direct forms of democracy. Others may use them for strategic reasons. A vote-maximising politician may, for example, adhere to norms of public participation to gain popularity. Politicians in opposition may use participatory forums as a way of rallying against a majority. Representatives from majority coalitions may try to use citizen participation in a manipulative way to legitimise a decision already taken.

At a general level, increased public participation is often presented as a response to a presumed crisis of representative democracy (e.g. Dryzek et al., 2019), where electoral participation is not regarded as being enough for the democratic system to be able to respond to current challenges, or for citizens to accept the burdens that the system demands of them. This is especially the case in local politics, where citizen participation is increasingly seen as normal practice (Michels & De Graaf, 2017). 'Democratic innovations' (Elstub & Escobar, 2019; Smith, 2009) is an umbrella term for various forms of citizen involvement inspired by participatory democracy (Pateman, 1970; Werner, 2020) and/or deliberative democracy (Fishkin, 2009; Grönlund et al., 2014; Mansbridge, 2019). These innovations can take on many forms and go by different labels such as deliberative mini-publics, citizen juries or assemblies, or forum for participatory budgeting, but have in common that they recognise the role of non-elected, non-experts in the decision-making process and often aim at providing policy recommendations of various strength (e.g. Pateman, 2012; Lafont, 2015; Setälä, 2017).

In Sweden, a frequently used format is 'citizen dialogue' (e.g. Soneryd & Lindh, 2019; Tahvilzadeh, 2015). This is a model put forth by the Swedish Association of Local Authorities and Regions (SALAR) in which groups of citizens meet with politicians and public officials to discuss specific political issues and policy proposals with the aim of finding common ground and solutions (SALAR, 2019; Tahvilzadeh, 2023). Typical examples are opportunities for public input on how a new district or park should be developed, but dialogues are also organised to discuss more sensitive topics like the spatial allocation of schools in a municipality.

The expectations of a more participatory way of organising democratic decision-making are often high, both among academics and governmental representatives (see e.g. Michels & De Graaf, 2010; Fung, 2015; OECD, 2020). By including citizens' perspectives in the process, the hope is to make the final policy decisions more acceptable to the public: either for instrumental reasons (the decision was good) or, as discussed in Chap. 3, because participants value fairness in decision-making. In a longer perspective, opportunities to participate and deliberate on political issues can also function as a form of school in democracy, fostering civic skills, and enlightenment. Similarly, by involving street-level professionals in the process, decision-makers will receive relevant considerations and arguments that are needed to make a proper decision and gain legitimacy. For example, Wänström (2015) argues in his study on school closures that the support from the teaching staff, who are often trusted by parents and relatives of the pupils, was essential as any arguments referring to the quality of education may easily lose their credibility if the professional educators—teachers—do not endorse the plans.

Considering all this, it is not surprising that ideals of increased public participation are met with interest and enthusiasm by democratically minded and politically interested people.

> **Managing Snow: A Nordic LULU Challenge**
> For countries and places in the north, snow may be beautiful, but it needs to be managed. It covers streets, parking lots, roof tops, and driveways—and it must be cleared for societies to function and for roofs not to collapse under heavy pressure. For this reason, snow dumps or snow disposal sites are utilised. These are designated areas where excess snow that has been cleared is piled up until it can be dealt with or melts away naturally when spring comes. Truckloads with snow to a single snow dump can number in the thousands, or even tens of thousands. There is essentially no limit to how big these can get—'It's a long way up to the sky,' a snow removal operator in Sweden stated (P4 Västerbotten, 2021) (Fig. 6.1).
>
> While these large snow piles at a distance may look like small white mountains and tempt children to play in them, they are filled with dirt, pollution, and harmful substances. Snow removal operations also generate traffic and noise from snowploughs and trucks. As snow melts, it can release unpleasant odours and lead to air and water pollution. For logistical reasons, these snow dumps must be placed close to central areas where need for snow removal is greatest, but they must also be kept at a distance from children, mischievous teenagers, and residential homes. This makes their placement a not-so-easy task.

(continued)

(continued)

Fig. 6.1 A snow dump. (*Note:* This is one of four snow dumps in Umeå, a mid-sized city in the north of Sweden. Photo by Louise Skoog)

WHY PUBLIC PARTICIPATION IS NOT NECESSARILY THE SOLUTION

Despite all theoretically grounded and presumed positive effects, people working with public participation often experience that it is not a straightforward road to public acceptance and legitimacy. There has also been internal criticism in the research field for failing to examine failures of democratic innovations (Spada & Ryan, 2017).

From a normative perspective, arrangements involving public participation in location decisions, whether initiated from decision-makers or citizenry, come with some well-known drawbacks. Notably, some participatory arrangements tend to give disproportionate influence to certain groups of individuals, thereby jeopardising the principle of equality that is inherent in the representative model where each citizen has one vote. In many cases, this means that people with more resources in terms of time, skills, and status will be more able to influence location decisions. For example, Larsson Taghizadeh (2016) shows that in the case of school closures, protesters mobilising high-income activists and activists with great analytical and civic skills are more likely to present policy-relevant information and to be successful in achieving their goals in the end. Similarly, Aldrich (2008) shows that areas with strong and high-capacity networks of citizens may not even be proposed as locations for controversial LULUs (or 'public bads' in his words) in the first place, as bureaucrats and decision-makers will anticipate dense protests that will delay or disable the projects. In other words, citizen participation can create opportunities for those with strong feelings and opinions, or as some would say, increase the influence for those who shout (or can be expected to shout) the loudest.

Moreover, there are practical problems. First, getting people to participate in location decision processes is not as easy as one might expect. Although many people are attracted to the idea of public participation in general (Christensen, 2020), and research shows that many citizens think that people like themselves have too little influence in politics (e.g. Renwick et al., 2022), many are reluctant to get actively involved themselves. When people work full-time, take care of children and elderly parents, making room in the calendar for political discussions about local development is not a priority. As a result, as noted by, for example, Luton (1993), it sometimes appears that primarily two groups of citizens participate when public authorities invite the public: those who have a strong personal interest, for example, to keep a LALU or prevent a LULU from being established in the neighbourhood, and those who take the opportunity to voice complaints about government in general—regardless of the matter at hand. A solution could be to enhance recruitment efforts to engage more 'average' residents, not just by announcing public meetings but through door-knocking campaigns for wider representation. However, such ambitious recruitment requires significant time and resources, and increases administrative tasks. These costs must be weighed against the benefits for participants and the community's well-being.

Second, establishing a functioning working climate for discussing location problems is a challenge. Outcome favourability, that is having it the way one prefers, has been shown to strongly influence public beliefs about decisions and decision-making procedures (Doherty & Wolak, 2012; Esaiasson et al., 2019). Therefore, many arrangements for increasing public influence—even the well organised and justified ones—risks ending up in chaotic argumentation or even personal attacks, rather than a respectful and creative strive for mutual ground and compromise. As shown by, for example, Fredriksson and Moberg (2018) studying public actions against decommissioning in local health services, members of the public often question not only the information and calculations that location decisions are based on but also the intentions of decision-makers, suggesting that they are inhumane and cowardly. In a similar way, Hendriks and Lees-Marshment (2019) found that political leaders often are frustrated by formal participatory arrangements, considering the input these generate to be uninformed, biased, and dominated by loud interest groups. Therefore, they prefer informal conversations with citizens.

An ambitious attempt to develop citizen dialogues in 'complex issues' led by the Swedish Association of Local Authorities and Regions (Hellquist & Westin, 2019) can serve as an example. Whereas several municipalities chose to organise their dialogues around open questions on how to secure well-being and safety of members in the community, one municipality chose to discuss the organisation of schools. Although they also tried to make this into an open question by asking what a high-quality school would look like, the discussion during the actual meetings was quickly directed towards a clear line of conflict among the participants: the preservation of village schools versus centralisation of the school organisation. In the end, all attempts to reach consensus were abandoned and separate alternatives were developed. This illustrates the challenges of using public participation as a way of building public legitimacy when the stakes are high.

Third, even if a conversation ends up in good manners, it may provide recommendations that are not easily implemented. Arrangements for public involvement in decision-making are typically not presented as alternatives to representative democracy. Rather, they are advisory complements to established democratic procedures (Germann et al., 2022). This means that politicians are, as elected representatives, in most cases formally allowed to disregard input from citizens via participatory forums (Nederhand & Edelenbos, 2023). Politicians are also generally sceptical about granting citizens formal power to decide on common matters (e.g. Koskimaa et al., 2024).

On the one hand, this can lead to worries that the decision-makers will engage in simple cherry-picking (e.g. Font et al., 2018), adhering to recommendations they like and ignoring the others. If such a narrative spreads, people may eventually be even less inclined to participate. On the other hand, an equally unfortunate situation may emerge if politicians feel pressured to make a decision that they do not agree with. As formal decision-making power lies with political representatives, this means that it is their responsibility that their decisions are ethically, practically, and economically viable. They are also the only ones that citizens who have not themselves participated can demand accountability from. If politicians feel that they cannot defend a location decision based on citizens' recommendations, they must have the courage to make a different decision. At the same time, empirical studies show that deviating from recommendations derived from a participatory process makes people perceive the process as being less legitimate (Germann et al., 2022; Van Dijk & Lefevere, 2023), thereby putting decision-makers in a delicate situation.

The case of referendums, as some would argue that these are the most democratic way of deciding on controversial cases, can serve to illustrate the situation. Sweden adopted a refined *Act on Enhanced People's Initiative* in 2011 that made it easier for the population to demand (advisory) referendums on local issues (SALAR, 2023). When Wänström (2015) analysed eight cases when the population had demanded a referendum on school reorganisations or closures, he found that the result of the referendums was in all cases that the schools should be preserved. However, in almost all the cases, the politicians decided against these recommendations. The argument was often that the need to reform school organisations was so great that the reforms would eventually be necessary anyway. Moreover, the reorganisation was often a piece of a larger puzzle to align resources with quality demands and it was difficult to break a particular decision out of that puzzle. Finally, electoral participation was, in many cases, low which meant that only a minority of the population was engaged in the issue. This shows that politicians can be prepared to decide against recommendations from the public, but they may have to pay the price of being accused of stinginess, deception, or manipulation.

All in all, this means that although the idea of public participation as a tool to bridge differences of opinion and grow legitimacy for painful location decisions is intuitively appealing, it is not an easy solution. It consumes resources and valuable time and may result in negative consequences both in substance and in terms of legitimacy. When and how to invite the public is therefore a question that needs careful contemplation by those who will, in the end, be responsible for decisions on location.

Summary

In this chapter, we have discussed how the democratic system handles decisions on location of public services. The legitimacy of the democratic system hinges on political leaders' ability to make decisions that reflect the interests of the public. At the same time, political representatives must have the courage to make bold decisions, such as unavoidable closures of valued service facilities, in situations of fiscal constraints and changing societal needs. They can try to avoid painful decisions by, for example, finding alternative ways of providing services or delaying them as long as possible, but at some points, actual prioritisations will most likely have to be made. In principle, these decisions can be reached by majority ruling or by trying to strike a compromise. These options have different consequences for accountability, transparency, and decision-making efficiency.

Perceived weaknesses of the political system's ability to handle location decisions have led to calls for increased direct involvement of the public in the decision-making process. While this strategy has clear benefits in theory, not least that it can promote perceived legitimacy by adhering to principles of procedural fairness, it has, however, also proved to come with significant disadvantages when it comes to political equality and the prospects of generating acceptance for necessary yet unpopular decisions.

References

Aldrich, D. P. (2008). *Site fights: Divisive facilities and civil society in Japan and the West*. Cornell University Press.
Arnstein, S. R. (1969). A ladder of citizen participation. *Journal of the American Institute of Planners, 35*(4), 216–224.
Bergh, A., Fink, G., & Öhrvall, R. (2017). More politicians, more corruption: Evidence form Swedish municipalities. *Public Choice, 172*, 483–500.
Broms, R., Dahlström, C., & Fazekas, M. (2019). Political competition and public procurement outcomes. *Comparative Political Studies, 52*(9), 1259–1292.
Chambers, S. (2004). Behind closed doors: Publicity, secrecy, and the quality of deliberation. *Journal of Political Philosophy, 12*(4), 389–410.
Christensen, H. S. (2020). How citizens evaluate participatory processes: A conjoint analysis. *European Political Science Review, 12*(2), 239–253.
Dahl, R. A. (1989). *Democracy and its critics*. Yale University Press.
de Fine Licht, J. (2020). The Janus face of transparency. In D. Mokrosinska (Ed.), *Transparency and secrecy in European democracies* (pp. 17–35). Routledge.
Doherty, D., & Wolak, J. (2012). When do the ends justify the means? Evaluating procedural fairness. *Political Behavior, 34*(2), 301–323.
Dryzek, J. S., et al. (2019). The crisis of democracy and the science of deliberation. *Science, 363*(6432), 1144–1146.
Elstub, S., & Escobar, O. (Eds.). (2019). *Handbook of democratic innovation and governance*. Edward Elgar Publishing.

Erlingsson, G. O., Bergh, A., & Sjölin, M. (2008). Public corruption in Swedish municipalities – Trouble looming the horizon? *Local Government Studies, 34*(5), 595–608.

Esaiasson, P., Persson, M., Gilljam, M., & Lindholm, T. (2019). Reconsidering the role of procedures for decision acceptance. *British Journal of Political Science, 49*(1), 291–314.

Fishkin, J. S. (2009). *When people speak.* Oxford University Press.

Font, J., Smith, G., Galais, C., & Alarcon, P. A. U. (2018). Cherry-picking participation: Explaining the fate of proposals from participatory processes. *European Journal of Political Research, 57*(3), 615–636.

Fredriksson, M., & Moberg, L. (2018). Costs will rather increase: Actions and arguments against decommissioning in local health services in Sweden. *Journal of Health Organization and Management, 32*(8), 943–961.

Fung, A. (2015). Putting the public back into governance: The challenges of citizen participation and its future. *Public Administration Review, 75*(4), 513–522.

Germann, M., Marien, S., & Muradova, L. (2022). Scaling up? Unpacking the effect of deliberative mini-publics on legitimacy perceptions. https://doi.org/10.1177/00323217221137444

Grönlund, K., Bächtiger, A., & Setälä, M. (Eds.). (2014). *Deliberative mini-publics: Involving citizens in the democratic process.* ECPR Press.

Hellquist, A., & Westin, M. (2019). *Medborgardialog om konfliktfyllda samhällsfrågor - konsensus, agonism eller mobilisering?* SWEDESD, Uppsala University.

Hendriks, C. M., & Lees-Marshment, J. (2019). Political leaders and public engagement: The hidden world of informal elite-citizen interaction. *Political Studies, 67*(3), 597–617.

Koskimaa, V., Rapeli, L., & Himmelroos, S. (2024). Decision-makers, advisers or educable subjects? Policymakers' perceptions of citizen participation in a Nordic democracy. *Governance, 37*(1), 261–279.

Lafont, C. (2015). Deliberation, participation, and democratic legitimacy: Should deliberative mini-publics shape public policy? *The Journal of Political Philosophy, 23*(1), 40–63.

Larsson Taghizadeh, J. (2016). *Power from below?: The impact of protests and lobbying on school closures in Sweden.* Doctoral dissertation, Uppsala University.

Leirset, E. (2021). Do open meetings affect deliberation? A comparative study of political meetings in two institutional settings. *Journal of Deliberative Democracy, 17*(1), 1–8.

Lijphart, A. (1999). *Patterns of democracy: Government forms and performance in thirty-six countries.* Yale University Press.

Luton, L. S. (1993). Citizen-administrator connections: Impacts on public facility-siting decision making. *Administration and Society, 25*(1), 114–134.

Mansbridge, J. (2009). A "selection" model of political representation. *Journal of Political Philosophy, 17*(4), 369–398.

Mansbridge, J. (2019). Recursive representation. In D. Castiglione & J. Pollak (Eds.), *Creating political presence: The new politics of democratic representation* (pp. 298–338). The University of Chicago Press.

Michels, A., & De Graaf, L. (2010). Examining citizen participation: Local participatory policy making and democracy. *Local Government Studies, 36*(4), 477–491.

Michels, A., & De Graaf, L. (2017). Examining citizen participation: Local participatory policy-making and democracy revisited. *Local Government Studies, 43*(6), 875–881.

Mokrosinska, D. (2023). *State secrecy and democracy: A philosophical inquiry.* Taylor and Francis.

Nederhand, J., & Edelenbos, J. (2023). Legitimate public participation: A Q methodology on the views of politicians. *Public Administration Review, 83*(3), 522–536.

OECD. (2020). *Innovative citizen participation and new democratic institutions: Catching the deliberative wave.* https://doi.org/10.1787/339306da-en

P4 Västerbotten. (2021). Redan rekordstor snötipp i Skellefteå. *Swedish Radio*, February 24. Retrieved March 21, 2024, from https://sverigesradio.se/artikel/redan-rekordstor-snotipp-i-skelleftea

Pateman, C. (1970). *Participation and democratic theory.* Cambridge University Press.

Pateman, C. (2012). Participatory democracy revisited. *Perspectives on Politics, 10*(1), 7–19.

Renwick, A., Lauderdale, B., Russel, M., & Cleaver, J. (2022). *What kind of democracy do people want? Results of a survey of the UK population.* The Constitution Unit, UCL.

SALAR. (2019). *Medborgardialog i komplexa frågor. Erfarenhet från utvecklingsarbete 2015-2018.*

SALAR. (2023). *Det förstärkta folkinitiativet: Trender och erfarenheter från folkinitiativ och folkomröstningar.*

Setälä, M. (2017). Connecting deliberative mini-publics to representative decision making. *European Journal of Political Research, 56*, 846–863.

Skoog, L., & Svensson, P. (2023). Hidden policy conflicts? Administrative strategies to manage depoliticisation. *Acta Politica, 58*(4), 819–836.

Smith, G. (2009). *Democratic innovations.* Cambridge University Press.

Soneryd, L., & Lindh, E. (2019). Citizen dialogue for whom? Competing rationalities in urban planning, the case of Gothenburg, Sweden. *Urban Research and Practice, 12*(3), 230–246.

Spada, P., & Ryan, M. (2017). The failure to examine failures in democratic innovation. *PS: Political Science and Politics, 50*(3), 772–778.

Steiner, J., Bächtiger, A., Spörndli, M., & Steensbergen, M. R. (2004). *Deliberative politics in action: Analyzing parliamentary discourse.* Cambridge University Press.

Tahvilzadeh, N. (2015). Understanding participatory governance arrangements in urban politics: Idealist and cynical perspectives on the politics of citizen dialogues in Göteborg, Sweden. *Urban Research and Practice, 8*(2), 238–254.

Tahvilzadeh, N. (2023). *Inkludering och medborgardeltagande – en forskningsöversikt om hur medborgardialoger kan inkludera marginaliserade grupper.* Sveriges Kommuner och Regioner.

Uba, K. (2016). Protest against school closures in Sweden. In L. Bosi, M. Giugni, & K. Uba (Eds.), *The consequences of social movements: People, policies and institutions.* Cambridge University Press.

Van Dijk, L., & Lefevere, J. (2023). Can the use of minipublics backfire? Examining how policy adoption shapes the effect of minipublics on political support among the general public. *European Journal of Political Research, 62*(1), 135–155.

Wänström, J. (2015). *Åtta skolexempel på lokal demokrati? – Folkomröstningar och politiskt ledarskap i arbetet med att reformera kommunala skolorganisationer.* Kommunforskningsprogrammets rapportserie, 26.

Warren, M. E., & Mansbridge, J. (2013). Deliberative negotiation. In J. Mansbridge & C. J. Martin (Eds.), *Negotiating agreement in politics: Report of the task force on negotiating in politics.* American Political Science Association.

Weaver, R. K. (1986). The politics of blame avoidance. *Journal of Public Policy, 6*(4), 371–398.

Werner, H. (2020). *Pragmatic citizens: A bottom-up perspective on participatory politics.* Doctoral dissertation, University of Amsterdam and KU Leuven.

Wittberg, E. (2023). *Corruption risks in a mature democracy: Mechanisms of social advantage and danger zones for corruption.* Doctoral dissertation, Linköping University Electronic Press.

Wolak, J. (2020). *Compromise in an age of party polarization.* Oxford University Press.

CHAPTER 7

Solutions

The location of public services and facilities essentially manifests the government's physical presence to citizens, influencing how they access benefits and responsibilities. Where and how people encounter representations of the public sector affects their perceptions of the government and sense of belonging to a society.

However, despite its significance, the academic world has largely overlooked the location of public services as a general political phenomenon and practical challenge in a democratic society, often concentrating on specific cases or types of service facilities instead. Our aim with this book has been to provide an overview of perspectives and hopefully a few insights into why location of public services is so crucial for people's lives and for the state of democracy.

In this concluding chapter, our point of departure is that political leaders must have the courage to make difficult and sometimes painful trade-off decisions when it comes to location of service facilities. Decisions on location are inherently complex, encompassing a multitude of, on the one hand, value conflicts and democratic processes and, on the other, regulations, budgetary constraints, and administrative frameworks. This means that it will never be possible to find solutions that everyone will agree on. Simply put: people will be disappointed. Legitimate interests will be underprioritised.

At the same time, decision-makers must seek to identify, if not solutions with unanimous support, then at least the 'least bad' options for managing the situation in a manner that gains legitimacy in the public's eyes. If not for all individuals, at least for a fair share. If not for all specific decisions, at least for most of them. And if not immediately, at least in the long run.

In the following, we will try to summarise the different perspectives brought up in the previous chapters into discussions on some potential solutions and broad recommendations on how a local democratic system that supports local political leaders in fulfilling their task should be designed. This involves embracing the location challenge as a political issue; managing people's expectations; ensuring a robust decision-making process through proper use of the administration; taking a long-term perspective into account; compensating for the inconveniences that location decisions may cause for some; maintaining an open yet critically evaluative attitude towards technical innovations and collaborative solutions; and, last but not least, designing public institutions capable of addressing the location challenge by establishing conditions for local democracy to function effectively.

As will become clear, most of these recommendations are by no means clear-cut prescriptions. Rather, they represent potential directions of intent which needs to be filled with contextual content. Thereby, they also represent avenues for future research. We end the chapter by presenting some suggestions for how the research field of location dilemmas can develop.

Embrace the Location Challenge as a Political Issue

Where LULUs and LALUs are located, and not located, risks generate societal conflicts and make emotions run hot in local communities. But avoiding conflicts by *not* making a decision is itself a decision. And this conflict avoidance strategy cannot go on forever; eventually, run-down service facilities must either be renovated or closed—or they risk collapsing.

A starting point for addressing the location challenge is therefore to recognise that, like other political issues, it almost always involves a choice between conflicting alternatives, inevitably favouring one interest over another. To embrace the political nature of location issues is not to undermine democracy; on the contrary, it is the first step towards allowing location issues to be contested within the democratic institutions. It is only through such efforts that we can manage the challenges faced by democratic systems (Mouffe, 2011). In representative democracies, political representatives must articulate their stances clearly and, when necessary, demonstrate to voters which compromises were made, which parties were involved, and which principles guided the decisions. This allows voters to hold decision-makers accountable and ensures that political parties represent the will of the public.

Unfortunately, there are indications that representative democracy, at least in the case of Sweden, may not be fully equipped to address these issues. As discussed in Chaps. 2 and 5, positions of political parties only partially reflect the underlying conflicts, providing voters with limited means to influence outcomes through voting. Engaged voters can, of course, take matters into their own hands and establish a new party. However, if these local parties become single-issue entities with a grievance profile, it is not necessarily a sign of strength for the system. Ideally, parties should have a broad set of positions on all relevant issues to enable accountability and be prepared to make tough but necessary decisions rather than merely communicating dissatisfaction. Moreover, even more concerning is the almost non-existent correlation between voters' party choices and their views on service location evident in Chap. 2, making it hard to interpret election results as indicative of public direction on these matters. These realisations may lead to a sense of pessimism about the democratic system's capacity to handle such intricate challenges.

So, what can be done? Our suggested path forward includes two main steps: firstly, democratic systems should embrace, not deny, political dissent on location issues. Resolutions should stem from discussions and debates wherein political actors are made aware of the consequences of each choice. These discussions should, however, be respectful. To promote legitimacy, political disagreements must take on a form that curbs antagonistic behaviour and does not threaten political stability (Mouffe, 2011; Skoog, 2019). Individuals engaged in politics at all levels of society must learn to respect those representing different opinions, viewing political adversaries as opponents—not enemies. In this context, democracy serves as a mechanism to establish a political culture that encourages civic engagement, endorses the manifestation of political conflicts, but ensures they are contained within well-defined boundaries (Diamond, 1990).

Secondly, political parties should be encouraged to adopt and maintain clear positions on matters concerning location of certain facilities, spatial allocation of services in general, and the delicate balance between decentralisation and centralisation. Parties should be prepared to defend these viewpoints, even if it means losing votes in upcoming elections. When political parties avoiding taking stances on controversial but pressing issues, this undermines the fundaments of representative democracy and risks pushing citizens towards anti-establishment or, in more extreme cases, anti-democratic groups. By offering clear choices that reflect viable solutions and encompass the broad spectrum of public opinion, political parties provide voters with tangible options.

Persuading political parties to take a clear stance on location issues even if it risks upsetting the public is, of course, difficult. But targeted efforts by activists, the media, and scholars might foster meaningful change. Hopefully, a growing awareness of public opinions and a more adequate positioning of parties on location issues will enable citizens to understand the logic behind political decisions and that—at times—compromises must be made. This brings us to the question of realistic expectations.

Induce Realistic Expectations

While not a crowd-pleasing statement, it is obvious that there is a need for more realistic expectations when it comes to location of public services and facilities. The strong public support for decentralised service provision and efforts to 'let the whole country thrive' should, of course, influence public policy, but these ambitions need to be put into perspective when it comes to costs and possibilities to maintain sufficient quality. This concerns both politicians and the public.

Politicians in areas struggling with depopulation and bleak future prospects will likely need to come to terms with the fact that they will, to some extent, have to administer cuts and down-sizing rather than expansion. As Syssner (2014, 2020) argues, we cannot take growth for granted. Rather, there will be places and municipalities that will shrink, where people will move away, and others will not replace them. This means that possibilities to keep service facilities in more remote parts of municipalities (and countries) will inevitably be reduced.

Today, there are few, if any, politicians who seek mandate for a plan to adapt to shrinkage. Instead, many local politicians adopt highly ambitious plans on how to attract new inhabitants to their territory by promoting tourism or give large companies attractive conditions for establishment and operation. At times they succeed, at least for a while. For example, parts of Sweden have taken advantage of the cold climate to establish facilities for endurance testing of cars or server halls. In many cases, however, ambitious projects initiated to attract new citizens and 'put the municipality on the map' (Daun, 2021) have become fiascos draining a municipality's budget. Similarly, unwanted services facilities (LULUs) cannot be hidden away from everyone, not even in a large and sparsely populated country such as Sweden. Even services such as prisons and nuclear plants need infrastructure and personnel. They cannot be placed in too remote areas.

Therefore, while it is only human to try to avoid uncomfortable decisions, and many politicians entered into politics because they had visionary ideas for a prosperous future, a more open and realistic debate on location of services is needed. Sometimes, the brave decision might be to abstain from overly rosy plans for the future.

Citizens, on the other hand, will have to do their part. For politicians to be willing to speak truth about the prospects for growth and to engage in tough prioritisations, they need to be secured a reasonable working environment. Citizens must not like everything politicians do, but they need to act with respect and have a respectful tone of the debate (e.g. Skoog, 2019). Politicians must be allowed to explore different alternatives and investigate the consequences. They must get the chance to be heard when explaining their reasoning behind decisions. They should never have to be subjected to insults, verbal attacks upon their persons, or threats of violence (e.g. Krook, 2020). A well-functioning representative democracy relies on good people willing to take on the task of being a political appointee (de Fine Licht & Esaiasson, 2023). If the political climate gets too harsh, we may end up with only opportunistic self-interested careerists in office.

For citizens to develop a deeper understanding of the complexities inherent to public service provision, a fair share of civic education is needed. Citizens need to be informed not only to be able to assert their rights but also to develop reasonable expectations and be able to contribute with creative solutions. This gives the media a pivotal role in equipping citizens with the requisite knowledge to engage meaningfully in location debates.

Whether current media outlets are up to the task is, however, questionable. Unfortunately, many media outlets are inclined to simplify and sensationalise their news stories (c.f. Ekström, 2020) to generate virality, instead of publishing complex or less sensational stories that require more work and deeper investigation. Headlines where unpopular decisions on, for example, welfare closures are sometimes simplified to the extent that decision-makers are vilified—why else would they be closing the beloved and much appreciated public indoor swimming pool? In addition, there are 'alternative media outlets' that capitalise on anti-elitism and populism, often found on the far-left and far-right fringes. These channels normally position themselves not only against those in power but also against established media by creating alternative narratives or simply accusing traditional media channels of spreading fake news (e.g. Carlson et al., 2021).

In light of these developments, there is a need for a continuous debate about media outlets and their democratic role, as well as ethical guidelines and strategies to counter-balance false narratives. Key principles are broad illumination from a wide range of perspectives and an intellectual curiosity about why governments make the decisions on location of public services that they do. Moreover, the importance of raising awareness among citizens about the origins and reliability of information cannot be stressed enough. On a legislative note, exploring the implementation of regulations to counter the spread of alternative facts could be considered. This, however, necessitates a delicate balance to uphold freedom of expression while curbing misinformation.

Secure Knowledge-Based Institutions and Due Administrative Processes

Throughout this book, we have referred to location decisions as both complex and inherently political. To make tough but wise decisions on location, political decision-makers need to be as fully informed as possible on the factual matters, legal framework, and relevant considerations involved in the case.

For a political representative in budgetary distress, it can feel tempting to cut on administration rather than to cut welfare establishments, both ideologically (because one cares about the core public business) and rhetorically (because voters will be less upset). We want to warn against too hasty decisions. Without doubt, cutting on administration can often be a fruitful strategy to reduce inefficiencies, indolence, and unnecessary rigid routines. In the long run, however, prioritisations that drain the administrative capacity can also result in efficiency loss or reduced capacity to deliver on the public assignment. For example, the Chief Executive Officer

(CEO) of a mid-sized Swedish municipality admitted that the municipality had now slimmed down all administrative operations—doing the same thing but with less and less allocated resources each year—to an extent that they had lost sight of the longer perspective (de Fine Licht & Skoog, 2023):

> We have been very clear that 'all hands and feet' should be protected in the welfare operations, regardless of if we're talking about teachers, nursing assistants, or such. So, what suffers is essentially all forms of administration. All investigations. All development personnel. When someone wants an investigation now, I almost panic. Because we have no one who can do it. I must do all things myself. It becomes an obstacle for development. How are we to become more efficient? When we have no one who really has the time to look at the issue from a longer perspective?

In other words, bureaucracy is not (always) the problem. In some cases, bureaucracy is absolutely necessary. Governments finding themselves in situations where location decisions are to be made need to secure that they have qualified personnel with high integrity that can support them with background information and contextual analysis. Striking a balance between administrative capacity and resources to practical operations in welfare is therefore essential to secure public legitimacy beyond the specific school building, library branch, or suggested recycling station. Although counterintuitive to some, investing in administration—when there is a need—can thus be the brave and visionary decision for a prosperous municipality.

Think Creatively Yet Critically About Technical Innovations

When investigating ways forward in location issues, solutions other than reducing service in remote areas or placing unwanted facilities in controversial locations need to be carefully considered. This includes the possibility that technical innovations can offer less expensive alternative ways of delivering service.

Digitalisation is a prime example where things are changing fast. In many places, citizens' face-to-face contacts with government have already, to a great extent, been replaced with websites, telephones, and AI-robots.

This is not least the case in Sweden which has come a fairly long way when it comes to digitalisation. In the future, digitalisation may very well be a move towards a virtual and thus a 'de-territorialized' government (Pollitt, 2012, p. 3), offering services to citizens regardless their place of how. In a parallel line of development, advancements in transportation technology, such as faster and more sustainable trains, cars, and airplanes, have significantly transformed the dynamics of travel, making journeys quicker and expanded the geographical scope of our mobility. This suggests that digital and technical solutions can provide access to (some) services even in remote places that might never had it before. If this helps to stem population decline, then services requiring the presence of public employees can also be maintained.

When considering technical innovations as potential solutions to location problems, it is however crucial to assert that the extent of this virtual and physical mobility is not all-encompassing, and it is improbable that it will ever achieve such status. Certain public services inherently require a physical presence, and for certain groups of vulnerable people—small children, elderly people, and people with disabilities—innovative solutions may not mean easier access to service but rather no service. Replacing face-to-face contacts with technical innovations may create new 'winners' and 'losers'. Moreover, we know from earlier studies that trust varies between geographical areas (McKay et al., 2023; Stein et al., 2021), and there is evidence from Germany on a potentially important mediator in this regard: distance to services. Stroppe (2023) have showed that long-term absence of services—so-called public service wastelands—could lead to decreased trust in government, which in turn spur geographical discontent. Or, as Pollitt argues (2012), face-to-face contacts between citizens and public authorities mean that we have the chance to *build trust* and legitimacy for governments. If digital solutions become too much of a norm, we may undermine the prospects of creating a sense of belonging to a society for parts of the citizenry.

All in all, technological advancements and digitalisation of public services represent an unstoppable development that offers solutions and fundamentally alters the conditions for addressing the location challenge. However, the problem of location will not go away. With new solutions come new challenges that we must be wary of. Not least, it is vital to assist citizens in becoming familiar with digital alternatives to accept various technical innovations as alternatives to face-to-face interaction.

Extend the Process Beyond the Actual Decision

As discussed in Chap. 3, the process is fundamental to grow public legitimacy for location decisions. As it will simply not be possible to make everyone satisfied with the substance of decisions where cherished service establishments are closed or unpopular facilities are placed, the procedure by which the decision is made holds a potential key to greater public acceptance (or at least tolerance).

Research on decision-making procedures typically focuses on the process *leading up* to a final decision. As outlined in Chap. 6, various forms of arrangements for public participation have grown in popularity as a way to generate public acceptance. By letting the public be a part of the decision-making process, the idea is that the final decision will be more acceptable to most people. However, as we have seen throughout the book, decisions on location of public services are difficult to reach consensus on. Even with a perfectly rule-based, transparent, and participatory process, there is a high risk of citizens on the losing side developing feelings of resentment when facing, for example, the closure of a valued service facility. To reconnect with these citizens, an extended perspective on the process that includes also *post*-decision procedural arrangements (de Fine Licht et al., 2022) might be beneficial.

In theory, post-decision procedural arrangements can include everything that happens after the decision has been taken, including how it is announced, justified, and implemented. To carefully explain why a decision has been made has shown positive effects on people's willingness to accept a decision but also on their evaluations of the decision-makers (e.g. Colquitt, 2001; Shaw et al., 2003; McGraw et al., 1995). Sincere explanation signals care and respect and can eliminate worst-case interpretations of the decision-makers' motives. Similarly, researchers like Boswell (2016) have begun to explore how public participation and deliberation in different forms can be organised in the implementation phase of policies. For example, Wänström (2013) shows how a dialogue about *how* a school closure should be done, rather than *whether* it should be done, can create a more positive conversational climate.

Having a plan for what happens after a controversial decision is made may sound self-evident, but it is far from always the case (e.g. Fogelholm et al., 2019; Berg & de Fine Licht, 2021). Instead of actually explaining their decisions, municipal representatives often simply refer to previous investigations. Similarly, they often fail to initiate a continued dialogue with the public. Rather, they are 'called out' by citizens to explain themselves. The aftermath of a controversial decision therefore represents a potentially underutilised opportunity for political representatives and public officials to reconnect with disappointed and outraged citizens that we believe can be further developed, both theoretically and in practice.

Compensate the Affected

In relation to post-decision processes, a radical (and often expensive) solution to implement necessary but unpopular location decisions is to compensate the affected citizens for their inconvenience, whether through monetary means or otherwise. Carried out wisely, we believe that compensations can be a piece in a puzzle to build legitimacy for location decisions.

As we have seen in Chap. 4, there is clear support in public opinion for offering financial assistance to, for example, individuals living near wind turbines, or alternatively, that municipalities should receive tax revenues from energy production within their borders (e.g. Garcia et al., 2016). The issue gained further relevance in the Swedish context when media reported that 'Finnish municipalities build schools with wind power money' (SVT, 2023). Unlike Swedish municipalities, their Finnish counterparts receive financial compensation in the form of tax income, which can be used to develop or maintain local welfare services. This has reportedly made Finnish municipalities much more receptive to wind farm establishments. Simply put, if governments need to site unwanted facilities, they can attempt to prevent or neutralise protests by opening their wallets. A similar strategy can, of course, be employed when attractive local facilities (LALUs) are closed or restricted. For example, a village losing its local school due to recruitment problems could be compensated with a newly built house that can serve as a hub for local associations.

It may seem cynical to offer affected citizens money, effectively 'bribing away' their legitimate grievances. If this strategy becomes the norm, the question will continually arise whether the manifested discontent with location decisions is genuine or merely a strategy to gain financial advantage. However, the strategy becomes more morally defensible when we consider what the establishment of a LULU or removal of a LALU represents in many people's minds. Such decisions are seen as part of a broader context concerning the future of the community, and then it logically follows that one decision which reduces the area's attractiveness could be compensated by another that enhances its appeal as a place to live. It could also be seen as a measure to rectify an injustice and create a perception of relative fairness in the locality. Moreover, by offering compensation, the decision-makers can signal care and respect for the affected.

An obvious downside of this type of compensation solutions is, of course, the increased costs involved, and it is not a given who should pay for these extra expenses and how much. However, an even more troubling issue emerges if compensation for the establishment of LULUs becomes the norm. There exists a significant risk that such facilities are consistently placed in areas inhabited by people with fewer resources, who may be in greater need of resource enhancement and therefore more willing to accept the nuisances or even dangers a LULU may present. This risk ties into the discussion on environmental injustice (e.g. Ashwood & MacTavish, 2016). This sort of 'LULU-dumping' is a clear equity issue that risks creating long-term societal divisions across the centre-periphery divide. Therefore, decision-makers need to carefully analyse the pros- and cons in a specific situation before proceeding with compensations.

Proceed with Caution in Collaborative Arrangements

As indicated in previous chapters, collaborations are in vogue and are often proposed as a solution for upholding service provision in peripheral areas. The drive to collaborate often springs from an aim to optimise resource utilisation—for instance, through the coordination or joint provision of services to achieve cost savings and scale efficiencies. And as it is costly for municipalities to both grow and shrink (Fjertorp, 2013), inter-municipal collaborations (IMC), as well as collaborations with private sector and non-profit organisations, are of interest for municipalities of all shapes and sizes.

Common collaborative partners for municipalities include their neighbouring municipalities. IMCs offer the opportunity to preserve the small size and flexibility of units while simultaneously reaping the benefits of economies of scale (e.g. Pano Puey et al., 2018). The aim can be to uphold service provision as well as to develop better—more enhanced—services to citizens, and to increase their ability to recruit personnel and expert functions (e.g. Erlingsson et al., 2021; Eythórsson et al., 2018; Meltzer & Kastberg Weichselberger, 2022). This approach, in some cases, serves to protect against the perceived threat of amalgamation reforms (Swianiewicz & Teles, 2018, p. 613).

While IMC is often promoted, critical voices are also raised. When local governments make decisions jointly and share services, functions, and processes, the relationship between citizens and their municipality is distorted (Spicer, 2017). This makes it harder for citizens to understand who makes decisions and why decisions were made, meaning that collaborations might struggle with accountability and democratic legitimacy (Gendźwiłł & Lackowska, 2018). In addition, a lot of work involving both administrative and political resources have been made in order to make an IMC a reality—which can result in lock-in effects where ending a collaboration can be difficult (Andersson, 2016). And as IMC almost by definition mean that portions of a municipality's autonomy are being handed over towards a collaborative arrangement, this can have radical long-term effects as it has the potential to slowly erode local self-government (e.g. Andersen & Pierre, 2010). While the benefits are often argued to be greater than the drawbacks, it is still a challenge one cannot disregard lightly.

Another form of service provision is public actors seeking collaboration with private and civil society organisations. Specifically, when municipalities—either solely or in IMCs—struggle to uphold services in remote areas, political actors often hope that local communities might 'take matters into their own hands' and take over service provision. Sometimes, municipalities offer local communities a sum of money if they perform maintenance of public facilities such as sports arenas and public indoor swimming pools. But at times, civil society mobilise to take on greater responsibilities for public services, for example by providing primary care, schools, and libraries. By partnering with local businesses and non-profit organisations, the public sector is believed to enhance its capacity to leverage local actors' experiences, thereby creating solutions tailored to the specific needs of the local population (e.g. Fenwick & Gibbon, 2016). However, as many remote communities also struggle with population decline and an ageing population, there is risk that such collaborations—as they demand community resources in terms of manpower and time—might be too big of a burden for local residents in the long run.

In conclusion, while a single IMC is not likely to challenge democratic legitimacy as a whole, extensive collaborations could ultimately lead to the development of an informal asymmetric government system, effectively resulting in institutional reform without public consultation or democratic approval. And with regard to collaborations with civil society, it is vital to bear in mind that while they may offer a solution for service provision, they must be given support and resources in order to thrive over time. Thus, we recommend that the decision to engage in collaborations should be a conscientious choice made by political actors and governments after careful consideration, not solely because it is fashionable.

DESIGN MULTILEVEL SYSTEMS THAT SUPPORT, NOT UNDERMINE, LOCAL DEMOCRACY

Much of what we have discussed in this chapter comes down to what we, as a society, want with local democracy. While certain solutions to the location challenge reside in the management of democratic decision-making processes and the involvement of—or collaboration between—various stakeholders, it is easy to overlook that the capacity to address challenges is rooted in the configuration of the government structure in its entirety. Although such structures are difficult to change, nothing is set in stone. Across Europe, ongoing efforts aim to adapt multilevel systems to future service demands (Galizzi et al., 2023; Baldersheim & Rose, 2010). In previous chapters, we have discussed how the design of a multilevel government system shapes the framework within which decisions regarding the location of services are made: the specific tier of government at which these decisions are enacted, the entities responsible for making them, and the extent of autonomy afforded to those decision-makers.

Therefore, a paramount recommendation for reformers of multilevel systems is to acknowledge the role that institutional solutions play in shaping future location challenges, ensuring that such decisions are viewed as legitimate by the public. This involves careful considerations on the balance between factors such as municipal size and capacity, the delineation between private and public sectors, variations in service provision, and the principle of equitability (e.g. Erlingsson & Ödalen, 2013). The design of multilevel systems in relation to these values will have far-reaching consequences, impacting the legitimacy of future public service location decisions for a very long time.

However, structural reforms come with their own intricate sets of legitimacy challenges and should ideally be subject to democratic processes, allowing affected citizens the opportunity to influence developments. Engaging citizens in such slow-moving, complex administrative reforms presents a significant challenge. Understandably, they are usually more concerned with immediate issues that directly affect them rather than with abstract institutional designs. At the same time, calls for institutional reform may at times originate from the public, without always being thoroughly considered. For example, there is sometimes a tendency to blame the system's configuration for cutbacks and centralisation solutions rather than the responsible decision-makers or the complex trade-offs they have to manage. This promotes the belief that radical institutional changes would offer simple solutions to complex problems.

Indeed, radical structural reforms may sometimes be necessary, but they are often much more challenging to implement than anticipated. If structural reasons related to demographic and economic changes underpin the developments, focusing solely on institutional reform might miss the mark. Misguided assumptions about cause and effect can lead reforms to fail in achieving their objectives, potentially introducing new problems instead. Against this background, we strongly recommend avoiding myopic decisions, such as reducing the scope of local self-governance to achieve national uniformity in service provision. Such actions could not only fail to address the underlying issues but also risk undermining the principles of democracy and local autonomy that these systems are designed to support.

If local self-governance is to be curtailed, for example, to meet public demands for enhanced equity and efficiency nationwide, local governments lose tools to influence their circumstances. Among their most crucial tools is the decision-making power over the location of services. The legitimacy of the entire political system will undoubtedly be questioned when citizens realise that no matter how efficiently public operations are conducted, they are unable to influence crucial decisions regarding the location of schools and hospitals. Citizens' dismay is likely to deepen further when decisions beyond their control concern not only the location of public services—critical as they are—but also more fundamentally impact their ability to shape the future of their local communities. Local self-governance is not in itself a solution to the challenge of location, but without it, the challenges become much harder, if not impossible, to manage. In an era where democracy as a form of governance is declining globally, it is imperative that we do not render individuals powerless.

We acknowledge that many of these suggested solutions are based on an almost idealistic view of how democracy can function in a society. The ideal democracy is a utopia. However, we should not let the perfect be the enemy of the good. By taking steps towards the goals we have outlined, representative democracy can hopefully be gradually strengthened. Research and journalism can contribute to exploring and disseminating knowledge about public opinion on location issues.

KEY AREAS FOR FUTURE RESEARCH ON THE LOCATION CHALLENGE

Our hope is that the overview of perspectives and possible solutions discussed in this book can inspire more researchers and students to delve into the exciting field of location of public services in a legitimacy perspective. Increasing knowledge about the location challenge, what shapes it, and how it can be managed, is perhaps the most important suggestion for a solution in itself. While we welcome all kinds of studies into this field, we have identified five areas where we specifically see a need for development:

The Decision-Making Perspective

As specified already in the introduction, we see a clear need for empirically based studies on how decision-makers navigate (and should navigate) issues related to location of public services. This does not mean that we should side with the decision-makers' perspective. We would even say that, at times, it is obvious that decisions on location have been made in a short-sighted manner, without careful risk analysis, and even by means of flawed processes. But while there is a comparatively established literature on protests and popular movements in relation to location of different services (e.g. Pasqualetti, 2013; Uba, 2016; Norris, 2002), there is so far comparatively little on how those ultimately responsible for the decisions and their effects perceive and manage these situations in the interplay between public opinions and other relevant concerns. We believe that the decision-making perspective is necessary to establish processes for managing location decisions and finding legitimate solutions in a normative/legal as well as empirical sense.

Since these are decisions that need to be made at elite level, we call for studies of perceptions and strategies within the group of politico-administrative decision-makers—among politicians, political parties, and the top administrators—and for studies on how they interact with and make use of input from members of the public, formally and informally.

Public Opinion Studies

In addition to a focus on the decision-makers' perspective, we also see a strong need for public opinion studies. In a democratic system, decision-makers are expected to take people's preferences into account. However, studies on public opinion regarding location issues, or even journalistic opinion polls, are exceedingly rare. It is challenging to demand that elected officials follow the will of the people if no one knows what the people think.

It is particularly important to examine how public opinion on location issues relates to people's views on other matters, especially trust in democracy. Increased dissatisfaction with location matters risks leading to declining legitimacy for public institutions, potentially contributing to place-based resentment. Therefore, it is desirable for opinions on location issues to be regularly monitored by independent researchers, who can help identify emerging trends, discern the direction of public sentiment, and detect changes early enough to allow for timely interventions.

Moreover, for an informed debate on location issues, not only are regular opinion polls necessary but also a deeper insight into the underlying perceptions. Future research could therefore significantly aid decision-makers by clarifying the structure of public opinion on these issues and identifying the factors that influence it. The complex nature of public opinion on location issues is indeed a challenge, but it also presents exciting questions that we believe can provide insights contributing to public opinion research more broadly.

Comparisons

While we see clear value in in-depth case-studies delving into specific contextual mechanisms, we specifically call for comparative studies exploring processes and consequences of location decisions. By comparative we refer both to studies that compare how different countries, regions, and municipalities manage issues related to location of services, and to studies that compare processes and relevant perspectives across different types of service facilities. We see room for qualitative comparisons based on a few cases and quantitative analyses of many cases, as well as for natural or vignette experiments.

By making comparisons across polities, we would be in a better position to see beyond preconceptions and explore unexpected trajectories. For example, by studying two or more cases when a typical LULU is established rather than focusing on one specific case, we may get new ideas about when and how popular resistance evolve and can be mitigated. Comparative designs can be based on, for instance, geographical conditions, such as densely populated versus sparsely populated parts of a country; socioeconomic variables, such as high versus low educated population;

political context, such as degrees and forms of political conflict and polarisation within decision-making bodies. However, from both a practical and theory-building perspective, we believe that a particularly valuable contribution would be comparative designs based on which different strategies—in substance or process—that have been adopted. That could, for example, imply to compare municipalities adopting a strategy of centralisation with municipalities opting for decentralisation of services, or comparing situations where public involvement is high to cases where the process is more closed.

Further, by studying different types of services not in themselves but rather *as cases of* location issues, decisions, conflicts, or challenges, we believe that the field can grow stronger by identifying general patterns as well as area-specific learnings that can be adopted and implemented elsewhere. This means that we see potential in studies that compare reactions and processes between different kinds of LULUs (e.g. airports, prisons, wind power, snow dumps, and solar power farms), different LALUs (e.g. public indoor swimming pools, schools, and libraries), and between LULUs and LALUs (e.g. wind power and schools).

Location Problems in a Time-Perspective

As discussed in Chap. 3, it is not obvious how we should assess legitimacy. Specifically, the question of time is elusive. It is obvious that in the immediate aftermath of a highly contested location decision, perceived legitimacy among the public, and especially among negatively affected groups, might be very low (if one made a poll). As previously discussed, this might also be the case even if the formal process has followed the protocol and even if relevant actors have been given a voice in the process. As times goes by, however, things might change. The decision itself might turn out to result in both more positive and more negative consequences than decision-makers and the public had foreseen, people might adapt and get used to new circumstances, or resentment might grow in magnitude if reinforced by further events.

Therefore, without suggesting a specific number of months or years, we believe that studies that follow up on contested location decisions after some time has passed can make valuable contributions to the field by tracing the mechanisms of legitimacy-creation (or destruction) also in the post-decision phase (de Fine Licht et al., 2022). Specifically, comparing cases with different kinds of post-decision attempts to reach out to the disappointed groups or involve citizens in dialogues on how to implement decisions in the most positive way would provide highly valuable insights to how location decisions can be managed when resentment remains after the formal decision is taken.

In doing this, particular attention should be paid also to situations when decision-makers opt to *not* make an active decision. For example, if they decide to *not* to close a LALU even when there was a lack of funds to keep it functioning optimally, this should also be considered a location decision that can be evaluated after some time has passed. Simply put: funds to sustain it must come from somewhere, but the question is from where and at what cost?

Conceptual and Theoretical Development

Finally, we see clear needs for further conceptual and theoretical development. At the outset of this book, we proposed a distinction between LULUs (locally unwanted land use) and LALUs (locally attractive land use) and argued that these qualities could be combined with an estimation of their degree of necessity for the population (Chap. 1, Fig. 1.1). Although providing a point of departure, this clearly represents a rough model to categorise location issues. Further work would be necessary to sort out different types of decision-making situations and generate testable hypotheses on public reactions and suitable strategies. Moreover, it is likely that perceptions of what constitutes a LALU and a LULU vary between both groups of citizens and contexts which provide opportunities to produce more refined categorisations and deeper understanding of what drives protests as well as tolerance of location decisions.

Further, it is evident that there is a growing interest among scholars worldwide in various aspects of the polarisation between geographical areas. This is important research by all accounts. However, we see the need for a conceptual development in this field. While researchers interested in geographic polarisation often build their work on an underlying idea of oppositional poles, or power dynamics, between places, there is great variety of concepts researchers employ to refer to this dynamic, for example the urban-rural divide. In this book, we have opted for using the concept of *the centre-periphery divide* for two reasons. First, the concept implies a power dynamic between geographical areas, where centres tend to have more political resources and abilities to assert influences than peripheries. Second, and perhaps where our approach most significantly diverges from other concepts, is the notion that the centre-periphery divide is not limited to urban and rural areas but can also manifest within cities or municipalities, for example between city centres and surrounding suburbs, as well as among various types of regions within a country. Although further research is essential to determine the viability of the centre-periphery divide as a concept, we firmly believe in its potential. We also recommend that scholars in the field continue to work towards updating and developing this and other relevant concepts concerning political conflicts and power imbalances between geographical areas.

* * *

All in all, working on this book has reinforced our conviction that the location challenge requires far more research than has been the case so far. These issues are of utmost importance for individual's ability to live and thrive in their place of residence, for how public organisations can best utilise their limited resources, and for maintaining the legitimacy of our democratic society in the eyes of its citizens.

We hope to see you, dear readers, out there in the field!

REFERENCES

Andersen, O. J., & Pierre, J. (2010). Exploring the strategic region: Rationality, context, and institutional collective action. *Urban Affairs Review, 46*(2), 218–240.

Andersson, J. (2016). *Locked-in collaboration.* Doctoral dissertation, University of Gothenburg.

Ashwood, L., & MacTavish, K. (2016). Tyranny of the majority and rural environmental injustice. *Journal of Rural Studies, 47*(Part A), 271–277.

Baldersheim, H., & Rose, L. E. (Eds.). (2010). *Territorial choice. The politics of boundaries and borders.* Palgrave Macmillan.

Berg, R., & de Fine Licht, J. (2021). *När kommunen sagt sitt. Efterprocessen vid kommunal vindkraftsetablering.* School of Public Administration, University of Gothenburg.

Boswell, J. (2016). Deliberating downstream: Countering democratic distortions in the policy process. *Perspectives on Politics, 14*(3), 724–737.

Carlson, M., Robinson, S., & Lewis, S. C. (2021). Digital press criticism: The symbolic dimensions of Donald Trump's assault on US journalists as the "enemy of the people". *Digital Journalism, 9*(6), 737–754.

Colquitt, J. A. (2001). On the dimensionality of organizational justice: A construct validation of a measure. *Journal of Applied Psychology, 86*(3), 386.

Daun, C. (2021). *Draksådd: om haverier och fiaskon när kommunen ska sättas på kartan*. Ordfront.
de Fine Licht, J., & Esaiasson, P. (2023). Att hantera svåra beslut – ett nödvändigt ont i den representativa demokratin. In *Hot mot det demokratiska samtalet – forskarantologi*. Sveriges Kommuner och Regioner.
de Fine Licht, J., & Skoog, L. (2023). *Sink or swim? The politics of prioritizing public service provision*. Paper presented at the ECPR General Conference, Prague.
de Fine Licht, J., Agerberg, M., & Esaiasson, P. (2022). "It's not over when it's over" – Post-decision arrangements and empirical legitimacy. *Journal of Public Administration Research and Theory, 32*(1), 183–199.
Diamond, L. (1990). Three paradoxes of democracy. *Journal of Democracy, 1*(3), 48–60.
Ekström, M. (2020). Vad är sanning i journalistiken? In E. Gardeström & L. Truedson (Eds.), *Sanning, förbannad lögn och journalistik* (pp. 37–55). Institutet för mediestudier.
Erlingsson, G. Ó., & Ödalen, J. (2013). How should local government be organised? Reflections from a Swedish perspective. *Local Government Studies, 39*(1), 22–46.
Erlingsson, G. Ó., Isaksson, Z., & Persson, B. (2021). *Mellankommunal samverkan: vad är känt om dess effekter? En inventering av kunskapsläget*. Kommuninvest.
Eythórsson, G. T., Kettunen, P., Klausen, J. E., & Sandberg, S. (2018). Reasons for inter-municipal cooperation: A comparative analysis of Finland, Iceland and Norway. In F. Teles & P. Swianiewicz (Eds.), *Inter-municipal cooperation in Europe. Governance and public management*. Palgrave Macmillan.
Fenwick, J., & Gibbon, J. (2016). Localism and the third sector: New relationships of public service? *Public Policy and Administration, 31*(3), 221–240.
Fjertorp, J. (2013). *Hur påverkas kommunernas ekonomi av befolkningsförändringar?* Nat-Kom/Kfi Rapport 17.
Fogelholm, P., de Fine Licht, J., & Esaiasson, P. (2019). *När beslutet fattats: en studie av kommuners hantering av skolnedläggningar*. School of Public Administration, University of Gothenburg.
Galizzi, G., Rota, S., & Sicilia, M. (2023). Local government amalgamations: State of the art and new ways forward. *Public Management Review, 25*, 1–23.
Garcia, J. H., Cherry, T. L., Kallbekken, S., & Torvanger, A. (2016). Willingness to accept local wind energy development: Does the compensation mechanism matter? *Energy Policy, 99*, 165–173.
Gendźwiłł, A., & Lackowska, M. (2018). A borrowed mandate? Democratic legitimacy of inter-municipal entities: A comparative analysis. In F. Teles & P. Swianiewicz (Eds.), *Inter-municipal cooperation in Europe: Institutions and governance* (pp. 57–77). Palgrave Macmillan.
Krook, M. L. (2020). *Violence against women in politics*. Oxford University Press.

McGraw, K. M., Best, S., & Timpone, R. (1995). "What They Say or What They Do?" The impact of elite explanation and policy outcomes on public opinion. *American Journal of Political Science, 39*, 53–74.
McKay, L., Jennings, W., & Stoker, G. (2023). What is the geography of trust? The urban-rural trust gap in global perspective. *Political Geography, 102*, 102863.
Meltzer, I., & Kastberg Weichselberger, G. (2022). *Fyra år med mellankommunala samarbeten..* Kommunforskning i Västsverige.
Mouffe, C. (2011). *On the political.* Routledge.
Norris, P. (2002). *Democratic phoenix: Reinventing political activism.* Cambridge University Press.
Pano Puey, E., Magre Ferran, J., & Puiggròs Mussons, C. (2018). Beyond size: Overcoming fragmentation by inter-municipal associations in Spain? The case of Catalonia. *International Review of Administrative Sciences, 84*(4), 639–658.
Pasqualetti, M. J. (2013). Opposing wind energy landscapes: A search for common cause. In K. S. Zimmerer (Ed.), *The new geographies of energy* (pp. 206–216). Routledge.
Pollitt, C. (2012). *New perspectives on public services: Place and technology.* Oxford University Press.
Shaw, J. C., Wild, E., & Colquitt, J. A. (2003). To justify or excuse?: A meta-analytic review of the effects of explanations. *Journal of Applied Psychology, 88*(3), 444.
Skoog, L. (2019). *Political conflicts: Dissent and antagonism among political parties in local government.* Doctoral dissertation, University of Gothenburg.
Spicer, Z. (2017). Bridging the accountability and transparency gap in inter-municipal collaboration. *Local Government Studies, 43*(3), 388–407.
Stein, J., Buck, M., & Bjørnå, H. (2021). The centre–periphery dimension and trust in politicians: The case of Norway. *Territory, Politics, Governance, 9*(1), 37–55.
Stroppe, A. K. (2023). Left behind in a public services wasteland? On the accessibility of public services and political trust. *Political Geography, 105*, 102905.
SVT. (2023, April 16). *Finska kommunen bygger skola för vindkraftspengar.*
Swianiewicz, P., & Teles, F. (2018). Inter-municipal cooperation in Europe: Introduction to the symposium. *International Review of Administrative Sciences, 84*(4), 613–618.
Syssner, J. (2014). *Politik för kommuner som krymper.* Linköping University Electronic Press.
Syssner, J. (2020). *Pathways to demographic adaptation: Perspectives on policy and planning in depopulating areas in Northern Europe.* Springer Nature.
Uba, K. (2016). Protest against school closures in Sweden. In L. Bosi, M. Giugni, & K. Uba (Eds.), *The consequences of social movements: People, policies and institutions.* Cambridge University Press.
Wänström, J. (2013). *Demokratisk förankring i skolnedläggningsprocesser. Förutsättningar för medborgardialog i en känsloladdad fråga.*

Index

A
Administrative capacity, 121
Alternative media outlets, 120
Amalgamation reforms, 57, 74, 75, 86
Asylum accommodation, 53
Asymmetric division of power, 74
Avoiding painful decisions, 98

B
Bureaucracy, 121

C
C/d-scale, 32, 89
Centralisation/decentralisation of public service responsibilities, vii, 15, 62
Centralisation/decentralisation of service facilities, vii, 25, 32
Central place theory, 74
Centre Party, 92
Centre-periphery divide, 5, 21, 22, 38, 82, 132
Citizen dialogue, 104, 108
Civil society, 69, 98
Cleavage theory (according to Lipset and Rokkan), 23, 82
Collaboration, 125
Comparative studies, 130
Compromise, 99
Conceptual and theoretical development, 132
Conflict, 9, 82, 99, 116
Consensual democracy, 100

D
Decision-makers' perspective, 15, 129
Democratic innovations, 104
Demos, 62
Devolution, 74
Digitalisation, 3, 122
Dimensions of location decisions, 12
Distance to services, 8, 122

E
Economies of scale, 26
Emotional connections to places, 8
Empirical legitimacy, 48
Environmental injustice, 125
Equitable service provision, 63

G
GAL-TAN scale, 84
Geographies of discontent, 24
Grocery stores, 13

I
Input legitimacy, 50
Inter-municipal collaborations (IMC), 125

K
KOLFU survey, 64

L
Ladder of citizen participation, 103
LALU, vii, 10, 48, 67, 81
Legitimacy, 6, 45, 109
 in terms of substance, 49, 102
Liberal Party, 92
Local parties, 85, 117
Local political level, 14–15
Local politicians, 14
Local self-governance, 62–65, 128
Location challenge, 4
Location decisions, vii, 5
Location of public services, vii
LULU, vii, 10, 53, 67, 81
LULU-dumping, 125

M
Majoritarian democracy, 100
Mass media, 119
Maternity wards, 1, 7
Multilevel governance (MLG), 65
Multilevel government, 62, 127

N
National equity, 62
Necessity of service facilities, 11
New Public Management (NPM), 68
NIMBY, 10, 12, 53
Non-governmental organisations (NGOs), 68
NOOMBY, 11
Normative legitimacy, 47

O
Outsourcing of public services, 68

P
Party conflict, 82, 117
Party polarisation, 82, 88
Party systems, 83
Place-based activists, 7
Places that matter, 24
Policy congruence between electorate and representatives, 89
Political parties, 9, 82, 85, 117
Political representatives, 8
Politics (of location decisions), 5
Populism, 120
Post-decision procedural arrangements, 123, 131
Procedural fairness, 50
Procedural legitimacy, 50, 102

Protests, 3, 10
Proximity to public services, 28
Public administrators, 6
Public indoor swimming pools (PISP), 86
Public opinion, 32, 129
Public or private responsibility for location decisions, 13
Public participation, 9, 103, 106–109
Public responsibilities, 69
Public service facility, vii
Public service wastelands, 24, 122

Q
Quality of public services, 29

R
Realistic expectations, 118–120
Referendum, 109
Representative democracy, 16, 50, 82, 106, 108
Resource deserts, 14
Rural consciousness, 24

S
Schools, 13, 29, 30, 34, 90, 91
Self-interest, 27
Service users, 27
Service variation, 62
Size of a polity, 72–73
Snow dump, 105
Sociotropic concerns, 31
SOM Survey, 32
Spatial allocation, vii, 25
Spatial equity, 26
Staffing, 26
Street-level professionals, 105
Structural reforms, 74, 127
Sweden Democrats, 84, 92
Sweden–the Swedish case, 16–17
Symbolic meaning of service facilities, 8
System capacity, 73

T
Technical innovations, 121
Territorial identity, 31
Throughput legitimacy, 50
Time-perspective, 131–132
Transparency in political decision-making, 101
Transportation technology, 122
Trust, 46

W
Wind power, 13, 34, 70, 124

SPRINGER NATURE

GPSR Compliance

The European Union's (EU) General Product Safety Regulation (GPSR) is a set of rules that requires consumer products to be safe and our obligations to ensure this.

If you have any concerns about our products, you can contact us on ProductSafety@springernature.com

In case Publisher is established outside the EU, the EU authorized representative is:

Springer Nature Customer Service Center GmbH
Europaplatz 3
69115 Heidelberg, Germany

The manufacturer's authorised representative in the EU is Springer Nature Customer Service Centre GmbH, Europaplatz 3, 69115 Heidelberg, Germany. If you have any concerns regarding our products, please contact ProductSafety@springernature.com

Printed and bound by CPI Group (UK) Ltd, Croydon, CR0 4YY
23/03/2026
02076355-0008